S0-BSX-755

"FACTUAL AND AFFECTING"
—*Kirkus Reviews*

On September 8, 1967, while fighting with Delta Company, Third Brigade, Duc Pho, Vietnam, Second Lieutenant Frederick Downs, Jr., had his left arm blown off and the rest of his body mutilated. He had stepped on the trigger of a land mine, and was then evacuated by helicopter.

AFTERMATH is the story of his journey back.

"THE KILLING ZONE, his first book, ended when Downs was gravely wounded. In this continuation he relates with vivid and unnerving prose his long and pain-suffused recovery. . . . An intimate and powerful memoir."
    —*Library Journal*

Berkley books by Frederick Downs, Jr.

AFTERMATH: A SOLDIER'S RETURN FROM VIETNAM
THE KILLING ZONE: MY LIFE IN THE VIETNAM WAR

Most Berkley Books are available at special quantity discounts for bulk purchases for sales promotions, premiums, fund raising, or educational use. Special books or book excerpts can also be created to fit specific needs.

For details, write or telephone Special Sales Markets, The Berkley Publishing Group, 200 Madison Avenue, New York, New York 10016; (212) 686-9820.

AFTERMATH

A SOLDIER'S RETURN FROM VIETNAM

FREDERICK DOWNS, JR.

BERKLEY BOOKS, NEW YORK

This Berkley book contains the complete
text of the original hardcover edition.
It has been completely reset in a typeface
designed for easy reading, and was printed
from new film.

AFTERMATH

A Berkley Book / published by arrangement with
W. W. Norton & Company

PRINTING HISTORY
W. W. Norton edition / February 1984
Berkley edition / January 1985

All rights reserved.
Copyright © 1984 by Frederick Downs, Jr.
This book may not be reproduced in whole or in part,
by mimeograph or any other means, without permission.
For information address: W. W. Norton & Company, Inc.,
500 Fifth Avenue, New York, New York 10110.

ISBN: 0-425-07564-8

A BERKLEY BOOK ® TM 757,375
Berkley Books are published by The Berkley Publishing Group,
200 Madison Avenue, New York, New York 10016.
The name "BERKLEY" and the stylized "B" with design
are trademarks belonging to Berkley Publishing Corporation.
PRINTED IN THE UNITED STATES OF AMERICA

ACKNOWLEDGMENTS

Writing is a lonely task, so this page is very important. I want especially to thank my wife, Mary Boston Downs, for having faith in me even during my dark moments.

I feel privileged to have had Ed Barber and his assistant, Cathy Kornovich, work on this book. Ed is from the old school of editing and that is a Godsend for a writer.

Curt Suplee is the man who convinced me I could write and then constructively criticized what I wrote. Without Curt, I would still be talking about writing instead of doing it.

Joel Swerdlow has been steadfast in his belief in my abilities and his help at the finish saved my sanity.

I thank Teri Jo Downs, my daughter, for the title and for her support.

I also want to thank Marty Ellen Rose, Jim Campbell, Rick Hansing, Peter Nye, Jerry and Leona Schecter, Ray and B. J. Blunt, and my other friends who gave me encouragement, belief, and help in many ways.

Because of these people and others unmentioned I am a very fortunate man.

This book is dedicated to

Lt. Robert S. Hutchinson, II, United States Army
Corporal James S. Yoder, United States Army
Colonel James F. Russell, United States Army

These men died while in the service of their
country. I miss them.

CONTENTS

PREFACE

In 1978 W. W. Norton published my book *The Killing Zone: My Life in the Vietnam War*. I wrote *The Killing Zone* because I wanted people to have a soldier's-eye view of the infantry war in Vietnam.

My last day of war was 11 January 1968. At 0745 hours on that morning, I stepped on a Bouncing Betty land mine. *The Killing Zone* ended at that point—I was done with war.

This book starts where *The Killing Zone* ended. It describes a different kind of conflict—what a wounded soldier must endure while he travels the long road home. Many of the names in this book have been changed to protect the privacy of the individuals involved.

Most of us who went to Vietnam are stronger than our contemporaries who didn't. Perhaps this story explains why. Perhaps this story will also explain why there are Vietnam soldiers who have lost their way.

CHAPTER 1

Intensive Care Ward

Second Surgical Field Hospital
Chu Lai, Vietnam
11 January–15 January 1968

The First Hour

My left arm lay across my stomach. I watched as the nurse picked it up, slid my wedding ring off its finger, unbuckled my watch, and twisted the bracelet away from its wrist.

She handed my jewelry to an orderly standing next to her. He held the pieces in his hand, not seeming to notice the blood.

The orderly handed the nurse a plastic bag into which she dropped the arm. I had watched her taking my jewelry off, wondering what would happen to it. The arm didn't look too mangled considering that a "Bouncing Betty" land mine (a mine that flies up out of the ground and explodes about waist high) had blown it off my body less than thirty minutes ago.

"Maybe it could be sewed back on," I thought. I prayed it could.

But I was kidding myself and I knew it. The arm might look intact, but my stump was a bloody mess. The white bone was splintered. It was sticking out of a stump seven inches long and I could tell that the elbow section for a couple of inches on both sides had disintegrated in the blast.

What the nurse had just dropped into the plastic bag—

1

my hand, wrist, and about three-quarters of my forearm—was gone forever.

A shiver passed through me. My mind and the head that held it seemed separated from the horror the rest of my body was experiencing.

I was lying on an operating table in the Second Surgical Field Hospital operating room, Chu Lai, Vietnam, a ten-minute helicopter ride from An Cuong, the village where I had stepped on the land mine, about ten kilometers north of My Lai. We had been working patrols from Landing Zone Uptight and the whole area was "hot." Fighting and booby traps were everywhere. It was a mess, even for Vietnam, and made worse by the civilians who were mixed in because they refused to leave the area, though ordered to.

The "Bouncing Betty" had burst from the ground and exploded a few inches from my left hip. My right arm was also severely damaged and my hips and legs lacerated.

The jungle fatigues I wore were in bloody rags but another nurse, no two!, were cutting them off with surgical scissors. I felt very tired.

"Name, rank, and serial number again, please."

Jesus, I had told the Red Cross lady that; why did she want it again?

"Second Lieutenant Frederick Downs, Jr., 05337689," I told her, lifting my head to look at her where she stood at the foot of my cot. She wasn't even writing. She was clutching a clipboard and a ballpoint pen as she stared at me with an expression that hovered between sorrow and scared determination.

Two doctors stood working on the upper part of my body. The wrinkles at the corners of their eyes above the masks made them look intense and their conversation was on their work.

"Who the hell tied this tourniquet?" the one on my left asked as he held my stump. I missed the answer, thinking of my medic who never did anything right.

A light grayness and haze kept pressing into my line of vision. I saw my Grandma Downs's farm in Indiana where I had spent much of my time growing up. Grandma stood in the yard dressed in red or pink. I couldn't tell which. Both were her favorite colors.

Grandpa Downs was walking down the gravel road. He was dressed in a flannel shirt and bib overalls, and had on knee-high gum boots. He must be coming back from doing chores over at the barn.

That's strange; Grandpa died in 1958.

A voice broke through the grayness.

"Name, rank, and serial number, Lieutenant?"

"What's wrong with your Goddamn ears? I told you that already."

There was activity all around me now. The doctor on my left cut down through my stump to an artery which he tied off.

"Damn," I thought. "I must be really zapped. I didn't even feel that."

I looked around the room. Men lay on cots, each circled by a team of doctors and nurses. "Oh yes, those men are my men, the five who were wounded with me. I remember two of them screaming."

"Goddamn lights are sure bright in here," I thought. "I wonder why they don't hurt my eyes."

Nothing hurt any longer. I hadn't felt much pain anyway, just a racing numbness that was like walking on a leg that had gone to sleep. But I didn't even feel that anymore.

Blood was everywhere. I had never seen so much blood.

There seemed to be more people around me now— nurses, orderlies, the Red Cross lady—all busy cutting my fatigues off, cleaning me, sticking needles and tubes into my body, and doing much else that I could not take in.

Then the thought hit me. I am dying. That's why so many

people are here. I fought the thought away. It came back through the cold haze.

I was scared of dying, but all was insidiously peaceful now. The activity around me faded, but the thought stayed, overshadowing, blotting everything out.

There was no sense of melodrama, just a sad feeling that death was coming now. I did not want to die, I wanted another chance. I wanted to go back in time just thirty minutes, only that far, and do it over, do it differently. "What a stupid move, going through that gate. A textbook situation for a booby trap and I fell for it."

"Lieutenant, what is your name, rank, and serial number?"

I thought I told her that already. She seemed very far away.

"I'm Second Lieutenant Frederick Downs, Jr., 05337689, First Platoon, Delta Company, Third Brigade, Fourth Division."

She asked me again.

I felt very tired.

But before I slept there was something I had to tell her. "Be sure and contact my brother. He is on the U.S.S._____"

They would never know.

My heart stopped beating and I died.

The First Day

The gray fog contained out-of-focus pictures, but I could not concentrate on making sense out of them. Instead, my brain fought to cope with a million nerve signals carrying a single message—pain. The pain was so intense and enveloping that tears flowed down my cheeks. I tried to lift my right arm to brush away the tears and relieve the deep ache coming from what I imagined must be a cramp.

A hot knife of unbearable pain shot up my arm as I started to move it. Simultaneously, the big terror flooded through my mind, filling me with despair. Then I remembered. My right arm and hand were torn to shreds. A thick bandage wound in a spiral covering both from my shoulder down to the hand where only two fingertips stuck out.

Without wanting to, but not able to stop, I lifted my head to look at my left arm and I saw a bandaged stump seven inches from my shoulder. My head slowly sank back as I raised my stump so I could continue to stare at it. I did not stare in disbelief because I knew it was true. I stared in fear.

This place where I lay was the intensive care ward of the Second Surgical Hospital in Chu Lai. It was a Quonset hut with a row of beds down each side. The nurse's desk was in the middle so a close eye could be kept on both rows of cots. Every cot contained severely wounded men just minutes or hours away from combat.

Our groans and cries were a continuous sound fluctuating in intensity as men lived through their war again and fought with the pain that gnawed continuously at their nerve ends. As the effects of the pain killer faded from a soldier's blood the crescendo of groans and sounds of suffering would gather in volume giving way to contact with raw, open flesh or deep inner pain.

Some finally began to scream. And they would scream until the nurses ran to administer a shot of morphine. The screams would then taper off to a muted, restless moan.

How the hell did I end up here? I had spent two years of my life as an infantryman. Two years learning how to use weapons and support units, learning tactics and leadership. Two years of learning how to be a soldier, to accomplish a mission. I loved it. Soldiering would be my life's work.

Five months in Vietnam had convinced me—this was a good decision. I had graduated from the 92nd OCS company at Fort Benning, Georgia, in February 1967. After work in an advanced infantry training company at Fort Gordon, Georgia, to gain experience as a second lieutenant, I received orders to report in early September for Vietnam.

Upon arriving, I had been assigned to the First Platoon of Delta Company, Third Brigade, Fourth Division, United States Army, Vietnam.

I was conscientious and hard working. I listened to the "old-timers" in the platoon. At twenty-three I might be the oldest man in the platoon but the only real time that counted was the time spent "in-country." Although the "old-timers" were only eighteen, nineteen, or twenty years old, they had survived combat.

Gradually I became an "old-timer" myself and our platoon gained a reputation as one of the best. We could fight the North Vietnamese Army up in the jungle of the Central Highlands or the Vietcong down in the open rice paddies along the coast in I Corps.

We could contend with anything—enemy soldiers, mines, booby traps, punji pits, leeches, snakes—anything the country or people challenged us with. We were "hard-core!"

And we could accomplish the mission. The mission for us in Vietnam was usually "Search and Destroy." Success was measured in kill ratios, weapons captured, and body counts. My platoon, Delta 1–6, led in all these categories. But to accomplish this we had to pay a price.

Most of my men had been wounded at least once, some twice. I had been shot twice and hit with shrapnel twice. Most of these wounds were minor and we either stayed in the field or were sent back out after a little time convalescing. Oh, I was a good soldier all right. We were good, all of us in the First Platoon, Delta Company.

But nothing had prepared me for this. I could not imagine life without a limb. These things happened to other people, not to me.

How would I do anything at all? I had been a complete human being physically. I had worked all my life on jobs using two hands. I had played football, run track, danced, done well in anything I put my mind to.

I was twenty-three years old. I had grown up on an Indiana farm and had gone to high school in Marshall, Illinois, a small farming community. All of the life I knew required two hands and a complete body. The only cripples I could remember were beggars, sad old men who worked at menial jobs, or schoolmates on crutches or strapped into braces because they had contracted polio before the vaccine was invented. Also in my mind were the deformed people I had seen at the side shows that traveled with carnivals through the Midwest. I was now like them.

I lowered my stump back to my side. No, I was not like them. Somehow I would be able to go back to my job as an infantry officer, leading men in combat. I had to. My men were there waiting for me.

Whether that thought was pure egotism or only a powerful desire to return to normality I could not tell, but I grasped that straw because I understood it.

Pain forced my attention to other parts of my body. As I became more aware, I realized tubes were running up my nose, and a tube was in my penis. Intravenous tubes were fixed in the upper part of my remaining arm, and blood ran from another tube into a needle in my leg.

The pain was so intense that I ached and tried to shift my body. But the effort caused even more pain.

My mouth was sandy dry. I swallowed convulsively trying to work up moisture. I was very uncomfortable, fragmented, unable to focus my eyes beyond two or three feet. My regular thought processes were interrupted constantly by the shorting-out effect caused by sharp, varying pain signals bouncing from so many areas of my body.

Shapes swam out of the fog as two young nurses approached. One of them leaned down.

"Hi, Lieutenant Downs. It's good to see you're awake. We know you are in pain, but we are doing everything we can to help you and one of us will be close by all the time."

I nodded weakly and more tears rolled down my cheeks at the relief of knowing I was safe in an American hospital. When I lay wounded on the trail I knew that if I could just hold on until I got to the hospital I would be safe. And now that belief was justified. I felt secure.

My God! Suddenly the dread of every soldier screamed through the fog: a land mine! Fearing what I would learn, I hoarsely asked the nurse to check and see if I still had my privates. She smiled, put her hand on my shoulder, and told me not to worry, that I was okay. Her easy answer brought on the start of my first good thought since awakening: "Not all is lost."

The nurse in fact had a very calming effect on me as she fussed around straightening sheets over my naked body, adjusting the tubes, and checking bandages and open wounds. Most soothing was her voice as she chatted on about what she was doing to me.

She was the first "round-eyed" woman I had seen in months. My emotions toward her and this place were complex. Being completely helpless and naked I felt vulnerable to the war a few hundred meters away. Yet the nurse provided a haven, making a place where I need not worry that a dink would kill me.

And yet—anything could happen. I looked over at the wall—the dinks were outside: I could practically smell them.

Completely unaware of what was going on inside my head, the nurse stroked my forehead.

Such peace.

I croaked out that I wanted a drink.

"No, Lieutenant, I'm afraid you can't have a drink because you are hurt inside and water may hurt you even more.

But I can wet some paper towels and you can suck on them to relieve that dryness in your mouth."

While she went for the wet towels I fought the pain again.

But, my God. It was so intense I cannot describe it. When the nurse returned I begged her to do something about the pain. Anything. I could not stand this.

She gave me a shot and I drifted into a limbo of pain mingled with terrible thoughts of the future with no arm. The pain shots could not overcome the pain. The pain swept on, taking rest, taking sleep, dominating all. There would be no restful sleep for months.

The Second Day

Sometime the next day two more shapes approached out of my fog of pain. A thrill of recognition and comradely love ran through me as Captain Sells stopped and stood close. Colonel Weir, the brigade commander, was next to him.

Captain Harold Sells had commanded Delta Company since its inception as part of the First Company of Fourteenth Infantry Battalion at Fort Lewis, Washington. The battalion had been shipped by boat to Vietnam in June 1967, as part of the Third Brigade of the 25th Division. But because of increasing hostile activity, General William C. Westmoreland, commander of U.S. forces in Vietnam, had been forced to assign the Third Brigade to work in a Fourth Division area. This caused confusion because in 1966 hostile activity had prompted Westmoreland to assign the Third Brigade of the Fourth Division to work in the 25th Division's area.

Rather than continue to mix up brigades on paper and reassign battalions to their rightful divisions, Westmoreland, on 1 August 1966, merely switched designations in the brigades, assigning them permanently to the divisions where they were already located.

Colonel Weir, the brigade commander, was a short, trim man who carried himself with the confidence of a combat leader. He was always concerned about the men in his brigade and took pains to see that they got the best equipment, supplies, and service available. I thought he was a good man and I liked him.

With Captain Sells and me it went deeper. The ordeal and stress of combat made all men in the line unit feel closer because we all shared the same deprivations.

Each one—officer and enlisted man, white, black, Mexican American, Puerto Rican, American Indian, Japanese American—was a shadow of the other man. We lived inches apart, ate the same twelve basic C-ration meals. Together we fired at our enemy and, sometimes, when bullets entered the enemy's body, we were united in partnership at his death.

Conversely, we trusted each other with our lives. We were one, whether on patrol on the jungle floor or under a canopy of leaves during the night when shadows and memories jitterbugged a schizophrenic dance or at the moment when we held each other soon after wounding or at death.

But some relationships were closer than others, like that between Captain Sells and me. He was twenty-six, three years older than I and about my size, five feet nine and a half inches tall, with a medium build and brown hair. He had received his commission from ROTC and the fact that his father had been killed fighting in Korea influenced, I think, the way he shouldered combat.

Captain Sells was a no-nonsense soldier. He demanded and expected each unit leader to toe the line and to be aware of the consequences of his actions. He believed that platoon leaders, platoon sergeants, squad leaders, fire-team leaders, and foot soldiers were a reflection of himself and his leadership, and was as hard on himself as he was on his men.

He also took the loss of each man personally. Whenever the company was in a stand-down after an operation, Captain Sells would work late into the night composing letters to the families of the dead. Each death, each maimed soldier, he said, robbed him of a part of himself. He had intended to make the military his career but he was changing his mind with every letter he wrote to a family back home.

It occurred to me that as long as he was a company commander of an infantry unit, his sleepless nights would never end. I used to think that on my next tour to Vietnam I would be doing the same thing, writing those letters back home because I would be a captain and in charge of my own company. I wondered how I would hold up.

But now—now my mind was confused. Part of it told me I could never return to combat—another part refused to admit defeat. It told me that I could go back to the field.

Seeing these two men standing by the side of my bed did a strange thing to me. Their green jungle fatigues, jungle boots, web gear, fatigue shirt sleeves rolled up—all flowed into the easy pattern of the soldier I had been yesterday. I yearned to be part of it again, to return to the familiar.

Another part of my mind was trying to think logically. I was pleasantly surprised. Why would they visit me? Who could command their units while they were away? I knew there were obvious answers but they remained elusive because burning waves of pain kept cutting into my thoughts.

I smiled and raised my head. The tube running up into my nose and down into my throat vibrated gently, creating a slight tickle. "Hi Captain Sells, Colonel Weir," I croaked. "It's good to see you."

Their faces showed the strain of controlling the pity, revulsion, and horror that struck everyone new to the intensive care ward.

In turn, I felt sorry for them having to be here. This was

a grim place. They must be embarrassed. They are whole and none of the men I could see around me would ever be whole again.

I knew I had never seen anything like this ward and I certainly had not been prepared for it. Of course in combat we saw Americans wounded and killed in many ugly ways, but the dead and wounded were quickly "dusted off"— taken out by helicopter. We knew that support groups in the base camps took care of those dead and wounded, but we were unfamiliar with the details. Body bags and hospital wards had not been part of infantry training.

The thought "it won't happen to me" recurs to a soldier. It is how a soldier must think, or he wouldn't be able to face deadly situations every day. If a soldier's belief in his invincibility starts to weaken, the soldier cannot act effectively. I had weakened six weeks back, on 22 November 1967, the day my platoon—Delta 1–6—was caught in the killing zone of a North Vietnamese Army ambush.

Yoder, my pointman, was killed. I was shot in the boot heel and the ammo packs on both hips; a bullet grazed my hand, rock chips and bullet fragments cut into my face, and I was knocked down by an explosion. The platoon was surrounded and cut off for a number of hours before the Third Platoon rescued us.

Afterward, we were numb with fear. As the platoon's leader I continued to function through the rest of the day but my fear of death overshadowed all loyalty to duty.

On patrol the next day we were still shaken; we moved only one hundred meters down a jungle trail in two hours. The ambush the day before had peeled back our belief in immortality to reveal that death could happen to us, and the odds were that it would.

Consequently, I was so cautious moving on the trail that we weren't accomplishing the mission. Not even repeated radio calls from Captain Sells, goading us along, had any effect.

Only when Porter, a black squad leader, took the point and bravely moved out were we able to regain our courage. Porter did what I was supposed to do; lead, set the example. I was afraid because of the ambush and this fear made me ineffective. When Porter's example galvanized me to action, I jumped forward to accompany him on the trail: A madness overcame me; I was willing to die by aggressive action rather than cower behind my fear. And this madness led finally to my downfall.

I resolved never to succumb to fear again, for it was debilitating to the spirit. Unfortunately, I overdid it, confusing fear with caution. I became so convinced of my invulnerability that I lost all caution and walked through a village gateway any basic trainee would have known not to enter.

And I paid for that arrogance by stepping on a Goddamn Bouncing Betty.

I was ashamed to have been so wrong that beautiful morning . . . was it only yesterday? And embarrassed to have these men who trusted my judgment see me now in this little horror room of a holding station for the city of the dead.

"Hello Fred, Colonel Weir picked me up in his chopper so we could both see how you're doing." Captain Sells paused through an uncomfortable moment.

Colonel Weir had lived up to his reputation. That he was here proved that to me. He was shorter than Captain Sells and had the sparse build that looked good on an infantryman. He would have been called "lean and mean" if he hadn't looked so fatherly. He searched for something to say.

"You've done a good job, Lieutenant. We're going to miss you."

"Thank you, sir, but you watch, I'll be okay. I can still hold a rifle with a hook when I get back."

Harold knew I needed to be reassured that I was still a

member of his company. I guess he thought a little ass chewing would assure me.

"Fred, you did a damn fool thing by going back up there. How many times have I told you not to go through gates, and especially that one for Pete's sake?"

"Yes, sir. I know I shouldn't have done it, but we had checked for booby traps so I thought it was safe. I was going to set up an ambush at the location but the dinks got there before us. Just proves I was right: It was a great spot for catching the enemy by surprise."

I felt so miserable physically and mentally that I didn't know what else to say.

But a cloud of responsibility cast a shadow over my tumbling thoughts.

"What about my men? How are they?"

"I haven't seen Bob yet but the surgeon tells me he might not lose his legs. Everyone in your platoon wants to know how you're doing. I pulled them back into a defensive position and Lieutenant Jordan will be taking over. They feel pretty bad about losing you and are taking it hard. I'll tell them you are doing okay."

"Good! Tell them I miss them and hated to leave."

A nurse stopped to whisper to Captain Sells and Colonel Weir. My body slumped weakly back. They nodded their heads to the nurse as I wondered why I was so tired. The strain of talking only a few minutes had exhausted me, and the omnipresent fog had suddenly grown thicker. I thought of my platoon.

After all these months the First Platoon was tight. We were the best combat unit in the brigade and I was their leader. They needed my leadership to help them stay alive and I needed their support to help me stay alive.

God, I was befuddled! The only solid thought was to return to the safety of my platoon. I depended on my platoon.

They depended on me. I needed them now to help me endure.

My attention was drawn again to the gray and green elongated figures floating next to me.

They had said goodbye and turned to go. I watched them through a haze, walking away, grateful that I would soon rejoin them.

Suddenly one of the figures turned back toward me. It was Captain Sells. He put his hand on my shoulder. "I'm glad you're alive, Fred. I'm, I'm, . . . I knew you could make it." He turned quickly and faded into the mist.

Emotions welled from my chest and tears filled my eyes. I was embarrassed to show emotion when I should be trying to show strength. Crying for any reason other than pain was alien to me. I had been keeping so many thoughts and feelings inside myself because I was a man and emotion would be a weakness, I believed, but I needed to express myself. There was a need within me to do *something*. Damn, it felt good to cry.

There were tears of relief, but also still the tears of pain. The pain was so high and so intense, I wondered if I would live through it. At times I thought my brain or heart would stop working, just give up.

This was not an absurd idea to me at the time. I had read of men tortured to death by the Nazis. At what time during the torture did these men die, I asked myself. I did not know the answer. I was afraid to know; perhaps I had already passed that point.

My universe revolved in four-hour segments. Every four hours I received a shot of morphine. Nothing was more important to me than that shot.

The periods between shots were of two types. One was the mechanical movement of time the way we determine the rotation of the earth; my other measure of time was pain. I used to pace myself against that rotation. After a shot of morphine the waves gently stroked my nervous system. I knew the pain was there, but I didn't care. The pain killer muted the waves of pain much as an oil slick calms the surface of a stormy sea.

But as the effects of the shot wore off, the waves grew, stirring and churning as the minutes ticked away. Finally the muted effect would wash completely away, leaving me trapped within a raging storm where all I could do was hang on and endure and endure, endure.

Nothing else would work. I could not scream. I could not strike out at an adversary; I could not use anger, logic, intelligence; I could not beg or plead. I could not run away, I could not hide, I could not relax.

Absolutely nothing would take the pain from my ripped, flayed, amputated body. Nothing except another shot of morphine.

The way out was death. I refused it.

As the hours passed away, I would start to beg the nurses for a shot, but their duty forbade any variation in the four-hour limit. They refused to give me a shot until the time measurement in *their* universe had marked four hours since my last one.

Morphine is addictive, an insidious seducer whose siren's call I eagerly responded to. The four hours had been determined by a medical body far removed from where I now lay. They knew the danger of the pain-killing drugs, but I wondered: Could they know what I was feeling? Given a choice I would have ignored all future consequences for the immediate suppression of pain.

As the drugs faded from my system, I would clench my teeth and roll my body from side to side, moaning in rhythm to the waves of pain, all the while trying to be brave, trying not to cry out or cause more trouble for the nurses. Something forged during my childhood monitored the way I dealt with those around me. After all, I was a man, a soldier, an officer—strong.

On the farm in Indiana we had been self-reliant. When times were bad, it did no good to bellyache; nothing would change. Any reward to be had would be earned only by hard work. Therefore, the only way to get through this was to fight my way through, through the pain and whatever else stood in my way.

Strangers Attended by Strangers

The ward at Chu Lai was surrealistic, wounded soldiers, strangers to one another, attended by strangers in a nightmarish world. We lay helpless in our beds knowing that no one would come during visiting hours. We were alone in a foreign place; worse yet, our own bodies were alien. Our fears and anxieties about wounds, loved ones, friends, and the future had no outlet, and so they twisted and leaped through our minds as we fought to reconcile what was happening to us. The morphine eased the pain, but it also distorted every rational thought, which in itself caused us to hallucinate. I had never experienced drugs before and was very disturbed and sometimes frightened by the incongruous things I saw happening with my eyes when, at the same time, my mind told me, "This is impossible."

But the greatest malevolence of the pain killer was its malignant effect on will power. I was in such poor physical and mental condition that at times I would catch myself relinquishing the struggle to fight.

"What's the use," I dully thought, "if the best I can become physically will always be less than I was?" Some part of my will to live acted as a watchdog, however, and as it sensed that resignation, it would prod me back into awareness, into life. At first I thought this also was part of my hallucinations but I came to see it as essential to survival. Men all around me were dying, and they always died shortly after they gave up.

People: Captain Sells, the platoon, family, friends; all who knew me would be ashamed if they figured I had given up. If they respected me that much I had a duty to discipline myself, not to disappoint them. It is a tough discipline.

But no man can control his thoughts all the time when his body is ruined and his spirit depleted. Nights were the worst owing to dark shadows and drug-induced sleep, times when the life force flickered closer to extinction.

One night an infantryman in the next cot cried to me, "Lieutenant, don't send me out! Don't send me out, I am afraid!"

Startled by his call to me, I fought through the web of drugged pain and willed myself back to command of my platoon; I imagined that he was one of my men. The intensive care ward was only a dream that I couldn't escape; the man next to me was real, one of my men. I had to protect him; it was my responsibility as platoon leader. I turned my head to him so I could say something to comfort him. My mouth was like cotton, sore and sticky, full of mucus, and the effort to speak caused me to gasp, tearing at my throat. I started to cough, which yanked the tubes in my body and stretched out all of my wounds. I cried out in agony and rolled from side to side because it was impossible to be still with so much pain sweeping over me.

The infantryman looked at me and said, "Sir, please don't send me out, okay?"

The night-duty nurse had reached my bed by now and had driven the morphine into me. As it worked, I calmed enough to listen to the pleas of the infantryman.

I turned to him and said, "Don't worry soldier, I'll be with you. I don't make anyone do anything I wouldn't do myself. I'll go out with you to show you it's safe. Don't worry." I lay staring at the ceiling wondering where I was. I should check my map.

The infantryman died that night. Waking, I became aware of a hushed bustle next to me as nurses, orderlies, and a doctor busied themselves with whatever chores they must perform when a patient dies. I had seen it before and knew what it meant. "I told you not to go without me, Goddamn it!" I yelled. "I told you I never made anybody do something I wouldn't do. It's not time! Fuck! What's going to happen to us?"

I was crying from the pain of opened wounds, the feeling of helplessness, and the frustration of losing another man. Christ! I had lost enough already. Someone turned from the dead infantryman's bed to give me a shot of pain killer and I drifted off to wander in a world of mutilated soldiers who could not speak or hear or comfort each other. We were together, but alone.

My time scheme took on another dimension. I vaguely realized that I was being hauled into the operating room after about every sixth pain shot. From the conversations around me I picked up several basic bits of information. A battle was being waged to save my legs and remaining arm. Also, at least two times every day the nurses and orderlies conducted the process known a debridement. The *American Heritage Dictionary* defines this painful process as "the surgical excision of dead and devitalized tissue and the removal of all foreign matter from a wound."

I define it as pure hell. Nothing can prepare a wounded soldier for debridement. First the tape over a wound must be removed. Even though the army paper tape was light and only slightly sticky, it pulled off a thin layer of skin cells each time. After the sixth or seventh time, the outer skin was gone, exposing new flesh underneath. When the tape was pulled off, the skin burned as if scalded.

Once the tape was off, the medicated cloth that was stuffed into the holes in my body was pulled out with a pair of forceps. Next the dead flesh, scabs, and foreign material blown in by the mine were pulled out and the wound was cleansed with disinfectant. My nerve ends screamed for relief but there was none until the wounds were once again stuffed full of sterilized cloth and retaped. Debridement was a kind of torture, but a necessary one since the gaping wounds had to heal from the inside, and therefore had to be kept open and clean. Debridement was the only way. So much filth clogged my wounds—filth from the mine, from my clothes and equipment that had been blown into me, and the dirt of the trail where I had fallen—that it was impossible to close the wounds completely. If my arm or legs got infected I would lose them for sure.

During one period of restless pain, a nurse told me that I was going to be moved to a larger hospital farther south where I could get better care.

I didn't care what they did with me. The pain was scrambling my mind. What did it matter where I was? The pain would be with me.

The nurse pulled back the single white sheet from my naked body and started to adjust the tubes in my body. She held my penis in one hand and gripped the catheter tube in the other. "Lieutenant, it may burn but I'm going to withdraw this tube from your penis."

I grunted assent, not really believing anything could get through the pain I was feeling. "Eeeyaaaaa," I yelled. As the nurse pulled the tube, it felt like my penis was on fire and being turned inside out.

"I'm sorry," the nurse told me, coiling up the tube. She looked down and smiled. "Don't worry, I haven't pulled one off yet."

She prepared to give me a shot. "I'm going to give you

some pain killer to help you through the move. You'll have to take a plane ride and it may be a little rough."

After the shot I floated uncaring, as the nurses and orderlies prepared me and others for the move. I heard a nurse ask the one who had given me the shot why I was being moved so quickly. I overheard her whispered answer.

"He shouldn't be moved yet but there are too many wounded coming in and we have to make room. I hope he makes it!"

"Fucking A," I thought to myself.

I was too doped up to recognize the aircraft we were parked next to, but I fantasized it to be a C-47, an old two-engine taildragger used in World War II. Romantic but unrealistic. The military would be using modern four-engine propeller-driven C-130s as medivacs. C-47s were too old for this kind of work.

We were stacked in tiers on bunks fastened to the fuselage and an air force nurse paced up and down the aisle checking on us. As the flight progressed, she obviously became very concerned about me. She thought I was dying, and I, too, felt something slipping away. But no, I wouldn't, not after making it this far. I became very weak and disoriented and remember thinking as I looked up at the nurse and the doctor that maybe I was in bad trouble after all. I was shaking violently from chills, and the wracking pain from everywhere on my body made me nauseous.

I was frightened, hanging on, but still losing my energy, my life force. The last thoughts I had as I lost consciousness were of my vulnerability to death.

CHAPTER 2

Intensive Care

85th Evacuation Hospital
Qui Nhon, Vietnam
16 January–26 January 1968

Hanging On

I regained consciousness in the intensive care ward of the 85th Evacuation Hospital in Qui Nhon, a coastal village one hundred kilometers south of Chu Lai. As I became aware of what was around me, two thoughts simultaneously affected my emotions—one surprise, the other satisfaction.

Surprise because I was in a hospital and severely wounded. During the first weeks, when coming out of sleep, I always wished to hurry to escape this hellish nightmare so full of pain. But when I did awake I was surprised to find that the pain, the wounds, and the nightmare were real. The satisfaction came from being alive. I shouldn't have hurried.

Even in the midst of pain, the joy of gaining another day uplifted my spirits. Something could be done for me if I just hung on. I wasn't sure *what* could be done, but I knew I would soon be going back to my platoon in Delta Company and to do that I needed to be healthy.

I was confident I would heal quickly. Surely the doctors could put my body back together if I could only stay alive.

I was pathetically wrong about both, of course, but with the drugs overlaying my consciousness and damping the pain, uncertainty, fear, hopelessness, and vulnerability, I would grasp at any straw, even if I had to invent it through wishful thinking.

After surprise and satisfaction came resignation that I was stuck, at least for a while. I looked around me to take stock of my new room.

My hospital cot was toward the middle of the ward opposite the nurse's desk. The ward was a Quonset hut, sort of like a big culvert pipe cut transversely in half with a door at each end, air conditioned, with a row of approximately twelve cots down each side. Lights hung from the ceiling. I craned my head back until I could see the tin wall behind me. I traced the wall with my eyes as it curved up over and down into the wall opposite me. There were window openings along the walls but I don't remember any light shining through them the whole time I was at Qui Nhon. The door at the end of the hut to my right led to another ward in another Quonset hut. The door to my left led to a Quonset hut housing the operating rooms.

The army's medical system is designed to move casualties away from the battlefield in stages. Way out in the boondocks near the temporary fire bases, there would be only a battalion battle surgeon and a few orderlies. The battalion surgeon's job was to take care of the wounded immediately until a dust-off could get them out. These medical personnel were located somewhere near the middle of a battle area, usually on a ridge or hilltop. The surgeon's operating room was a tent with a wooden floor made of ammunition boxes. A wall of sandbags around the tent provided the only protection during an attack.

The next step back was a surgical unit. They were located at main base camps or secured areas. They were like the MASH units used in Korea, large tents with wooden floors and wooden walls about waist high. The rest of the wall and the roof were canvas. The second Surgical Hospital at Chu Lai had been of this sort.

Helicopter pads were located next to the surgical units. Dust-offs would bring soldiers from the battlefield to the surgical units where teams would be waiting. The surgical team's job was to stabilize the patient until he could be moved to the next stage, the evacuation hospital. That's where I was now, at the 85th Evac.

An evacuation hospital first continues life-saving or limb-saving operations; if that part of it works, then the medical staff determines the seriousness of the wounds, whether the soldier could return to duty or not and, from that determination, either has him transferred to a convalescent hospital nearby, or begins to map a hospital route back to the United States.

I didn't know any of this yet. I only knew I was in a crummy Quonset hut lying on a piece of canvas supported by a frame connected to a rod at the foot of the cot and a rod at the head of the cot. I was in a special bed known as a stryker frame. I would find out why shortly.

I had always taken my body for granted. It did what I wanted no matter how much I abused it in sports, working, or just being careless. But five days after the Bouncing Betty it was different. My body had suffered too much. I was worried and scared; I frequently fixed my gaze on the bandaged stump where my left arm used to be, going from that side to the bulky bandaged right arm and hand. Under the bandage a fire burned on my right arm up to the wrist, but beyond the wrist there was only a frightening void—no feeling at all.

Beyond what I could see was the pain from parts of my body that I could not see. In some ways that was the worst because my imagination saw a different mutilation every time I thought about my back, buttocks, legs, and feet. I was beginning to realize how seriously I was wounded.

I lay on the canvas cot with only a sheet covering my naked body. After assessing my body, I bitterly realized that I could not perform even the simple function of lifting the sheet so as to see the front of my body, to look for wounds on my chest, stomach, or the front of my legs.

"Fred, it's a lick; you fucked up beyond all belief!" I thought to myself. "You have no hands, so you can't even hold something to read to take your mind off of the pain. You had better do something to distract yourself."

About all I could do was sing "The Blue-Tail Fly." That would do it. I concentrated hard on that song and I should have realized how drugged up I was when I began to feel I had a hell of a good voice, sounded great. I would entertain not only myself but also the nurses and soldiers around me.

Suddenly I came to know that there were tubes in me. This sudden stab of attentiveness happened a lot. A quick, fleeting clarity would grab my attention and highlight a detail that only a few seconds before had gone unnoticed.

Then the alertness would fade away. I didn't question it. There was no reason to. So many physical changes had been laid on me that the mental aberrations might be natural, just part of it all.

I continued my examination.

Whole blood, blood plasma, and a third and fourth bottle of fluid were connected to me by tubes running into my feet and legs. No tube now in my penis, though. For that I was thankful. But those other tubes, what were they for? My concentration on the bottles of fluid caused me to remember I hadn't eaten since my C-ration breakfast outside the village where I had been wounded. "Why, I haven't eaten for almost a week," I thought. My awareness faded before I could connect the bottles of intravenous fluid and no meals.

For the second time since arriving "in-country" I was in

an air-conditioned room and shivering uncontrollably from the cold. The sheet gave no warmth. But most of the cold resulted from the tremendous amount of blood I had lost and my overall weakened condition. I was cold all of the time. "Just one more miserable, fucking, Goddamn aggravation to contend with," I thought ruefully.

A nurse walking on patrol down the aisle saw that I was conscious. "Hello, Lieutenant Downs. It's good to see you're back with us. You came in here looking pretty bad, even for an infantry lieutenant. The air force always tries to hit all the bumps for you army types." She smiled and stopped next to my bed.

"I don't think the pilot missed any, that's for sure. Say! I'm awfully cold. Could I have a blanket?"

"Sure." She pulled a blanket from somewhere and gently laid it across me. "My name's Lara. If you need anything our desk is right there, so just holler."

For the first time since I had been wounded, five days ago, I was able to concentrate on something besides my pain. I looked up into Lara's face and saw that she had brown hair and brown eyes. But most of all I saw the compassion in her face and for just a moment I thought very clearly, "She is too young to be over here and too vulnerable. She is not hardened to this yet."

I smiled back at her and told her I felt too bad to holler very loud so I hoped her ears were good. "Yes, excellent ears, Lieutenant," she said, tucking in a corner of the sheet and moving to the man next to me on the left.

I studied her body, which was very feminine, and vaguely wondered why I didn't feel desire, or worse yet, did not care.

Once I was more or less out of danger, I was nevertheless very uncomfortable from the pain in my hips, buttocks, and legs. To relieve it, I twisted my body into odd angles, taking pressure off my lower body, which hurt desperately on the backside, and then off my upper body, which ached from cramps. With the help of the nurses and orderlies blocking and supporting my body at different places with pillows, I was able to reach a degree of discomfort that I could endure. If I couldn't relax, at least I felt better.

But the hospital had its own routine, and there was a big surprise for me. No sooner had I achieved a good position than two orderlies came down the aisle. It was time to flip me, I was told.

Perplexed, I gritted my teeth as the pillows were pulled out and I was forced to lie flat on my back. I then learned the nature of the strange cot I was lying on. The orderlies took a canvas frame exactly like the one I was on, held it above me, and fitted the holes in the frame into the vertical rods at the foot and head of my cot. Then they lowered the canvas frame down the rod until it fitted snugly over my face, chest, and lower body. I was like a piece of luncheon meat between two slices of bread. An opening in the canvas freed my eyes and mouth, and there was also an opening for my penis. I would find out about that later.

"All right, Lieutenant. Now you must keep your stump and your arm tight to your side because we are going to turn you over so that you'll be lying on your stomach. The canvas on top of you now will become your new cot when you are turned."

"What the hell . . . you guys sure you know what you're doing? Are you shitting me?"

They laughed. "No sweat, sir. Really! It's the best thing for you. Your injuries are so severe that you must be rotated every four hours to relieve the pressure."

"And it makes it easier to work on you," Lara reassured me.

"All right, I guess the army wouldn't waste training on a bunch of bullshitters, but don't spin me too fast until I get the hang of this thing." As doped up as I was the idea of moving fast made me dizzy.

An orderly stood at each end of my cot. They inserted cranks into slots and unlocked the cot, releasing it to pivot between the two vertical rods.

I could tell this must have been the highlight of the day for the two orderlies. They rocked me gently back and forth and warned me they would count three and then turn me.

Watching the orderly bend over to grasp the crank, the thought flashed through to me that the orderly had gone crazy. He thought I was a Model T Ford. If I didn't start on the first turn, he would keep cranking until I did start.

At the count of three it happened just the way they said it would. I was turned and lying on my stomach, as the orderlies locked the cot into place, removed the canvas frame from my back, and replaced my sheet.

A canvas strip across my forehead supported my head as I stared helplessly at the concrete floor and wondered what in God's name I was to do with my life.

Then I received a shot and began to float in my wonderful world of uncaring. I could control that world and intertwine what was happening in it with the other world, the one people call real; these worlds blurred together and I existed in both of them simultaneously.

Staring at the floor, I noticed a strange pattern of movement. All of the tiny rocks embedded in the cement floor had grown six legs and formed geometric patterns and began to dance. Fully conscious, I realized that this couldn't be happening, but the spiders seemed so real. They must exist. It was easy to accept. Moreover, I could control the rock spiders. They did whatever I commanded them to do. Control was strongest for the first few hours after my shot so I exercised my mind by developing intricate routines for them to move into. They reminded me of an overhead camera shot of the June Taylor Dancers on the "Jackie Gleason Show" I used to watch in the 1950s. The rock spiders imitated those dancers by moving around the floor like a dully colored kaleidoscope.

Luckily, the flipping of the cot coincided with the pain killer, enabling me to transfer my visions to another medium.

When I was flipped onto my back and received the shot, I would concentrate on the shadows that played against the ceiling. The ceiling was better than the floor because it afforded more creativity, an infinite number of projections.

I would stare at the shadows until I controlled them. Then I could form them into any shape I wished and conduct a play in full color. They were beautiful renditions of episodes from my childhood.

Occasionally I would lose control. The witchcraft I was practicing would turn against me. If I were lying on my stomach when possession occurred the rock spiders scurried about trying to build a menacing pyramid up toward me from the floor. I feared they would succeed. As the pyramid of spiders grew, I would try to move my body away but I was trapped by immobility. Sweat dripped from my face as I struggled to destroy the pyramids, forcing my will against whatever power had wrestled them from me. Grunts and low animal noises emanated from me in such volume at times that one of the medical people would come over to check me out. Their feet sometimes knocked down the pyramids and saved me.

The spiders were scary, but the shadows were terrifying. Whenever I lost control of the ceiling a much more ominous vision occurred. The shadows would lose their bright colors and individuality. They would slowly darken and gather into a black and massive thundercloud, always the large and brutish head and shoulders of a man whose chest was a whirlpool or cyclone that pulled me into destruction, and nothingness. The whole ward would turn black.

On especially bad days the maelstrom blotted out everything in the ward as it drew closer to me. No matter how frightened I was, I never cried out for help. It would have done no good. This was a private battle between the chaos and me. I had created the maelstrom and I would control it. But there were times when it seemed much stronger than I, which was crazy. If it destroyed me it would destroy itself. It gained its power from me. It existed only because I was alive.

Even though I was conscious, the two worlds—the ward and my fantasies—existed side by side. Both seemed as real as any reality in my experience. I did not understand it and no one explained it to me.

Perhaps there was no need to explain. Surely others in the ward were seeing what I had created. But I was clever, devious. I never said anything to them because it might confuse them, or they might think I was "dinky-dow," the Vietnamese word for crazy.

The People Around Me

There was the other world, though, the real world populated by real people—doctors, nurses, orderlies, Red Cross volunteers. They were concerned with caring for many wounded men. I watched them and what they did. In the jungle I had had a tough job, but not as tough as the jobs these people performed.

On the battlefield we had no time for the wounded. I had sent them back, had them "dusted off" to a place where they would be cared for. But I had never wondered what that place was like. Until now I had never comprehended the meaning of purgatory. This place had to be close to what the religious philosophers had envisioned.

I wondered what the people who worked here were like.

One of the male orderlies was from Wyoming and as he cleaned our bodies he would tell us about the ranch he grew up on. He seemed to be a very sensitive young man and I wondered what he was doing in this ward of death.

Another male orderly was a wizard with cards. He would come into the ward on his own time and go from bed to bed performing tricks. Whenever we saw him come through the door flashing his grin and shuffling a deck of cards we would call his name, happy that he was going to entertain us.

His tricks were joyful, a delight, a release from pain and boredom. He did not represent death, or battle. He represented magic, relaxation, a reminder of good times back home, in "The World," the "Real Place" from which we had come and to which we were now returning.

I was more aware of what was going on around me in this ward than I was in Chu Lai's Second Surgical Ward. The staff here worked twelve-hour shifts unless there was a battle going on and casualties were being flown in. During those times they just kept working until the battle was over. The nurses and orderlies were constantly on the go as they moved from cot to cot administering to each of us.

Despite my admiration for these angels of mercy I dreaded the times when they were to work on me. My blood plasma tube and other intravenous tubes had to be changed every few hours. A constant eye had to be kept on those tubes to make sure everything was functioning correctly. I was rotated every four hours. I took a multitude of pills four times a day. I had a pain shot every four hours. I needed to have my pillows adjusted often along my body. I needed help whenever I wanted to urinate because a gigantic bandage covered my remaining arm and hand making it impossible for me to handle myself. In fact, I hated urinating. It was mortifying. If I was lying on my back, an orderly would position a urine bottle between my legs and I would try to pee while lying down in defiance of gravity. I couldn't exactly feel anything so I would get the sneaking suspicion that the bottle had slipped away and I was afraid I would pee on the bed. It took a tremendous amount of concentration finally to force my bladder to let go.

On my stomach it was even worse. Then an orderly squatted down next to the cot, reached up through a hole in the canvas, fished around for my penis, pulled it down through the hole, and held it up to a bottle for me. I would then lie with my head supported by the canvas strap across my forehead staring at the floor wondering where the hell the spiders were when I needed them. They could have taken my mind off the indignity of it all. Urinating soon became the great symbol of my total helplessness.

Many soldiers were in worse shape than I and their wounds demanded even more of the nurses' and orderlies' time.

A number of the men had chest wounds. These were particularly nasty when a lung had collapsed or partially collapsed. In these cases a slit was cut through the rib cage so that a tube could be inserted into the chest cavity to suck out the accumulated debris and to reduce air pressure in the upper diaphragm. Then the lung could inflate again.

If a wound was a "through and through," meaning that a projectile (bullet or shrapnel) had gone completely through the chest cavity, the soldier would have the entrance and exit wounds plus the surgical slit to contend with.

These men had to sit up in bed continuously to keep the fluids from backing up into their lungs. Each type of wound had its own set of problems with which the soldier had to cope. The chest wound meant that every breath stretched torn flesh; therefore, these patients always seemed to breathe very gently. The greater the damage inside the chest, the less the man attempted any movement.

But every couple of hours, just when a man would have settled into a slow, easy breathing pattern, a nurse would pull a suction machine up next to his bed and insert a tube into the surgical slit to suck out the debris.

The movement of the tube through the slit must have been very painful in itself, but the chain reaction the process started was something the "lungers" hated.

Irritation of the open nerve ends would cause the soldier to tense up. As the tube was inserted and the machine was started, the body would react. Pain would cause a sharper intake of breath. The pain of straining the wounds would bring forth a low animal moan, tears would run down his face, and he would start coughing and gagging, which intensified the pain he already suffered.

I watched the man across from me. He would be sitting up, his naked torso pale where his fatigue shirt had protected it from the sun. A bandage encircled his chest. As the time approached for his treatment he would begin to fidget.

The sound of coughing and gagging marked the nurse's progress around the ward as she trundled her machine from chest wound to chest wound. The apprehension showed on his face. Finally it would be his turn.

The machine sat on its cart to the right of his bed. As the nurse adjusted his bandage, there would be a grunt from him when she slid the tube between his ribs. An orderly would turn the machine on. The top was a clear plastic chamber into which a red froth swirled around as the machine sucked the chest cavity clean.

Meanwhile, the soldier's face was clenched into deep wrinkles of pain as he half sobbed and half coughed at the same time. His fists were tight knuckles of flesh at the ends of his tanned arms, which he held tautly against the bed struggling not to cough. The nurse would wipe his brow and do other things in an effort to comfort him. It was all she could do.

Finally, his ordeal was over, the equipment was removed and moved to the next chest patient. The man would collapse exhausted against the sweat-stained sheet.

I used the sound of the coughing and gagging to mark the nurse's progress around the ward.

The burn cases were in a special class. They certainly demanded much from the medical staff.

The soldier catty-corner from me was burned completely in the front from his head to his ankles. His boots had protected his feet. He was sitting up with his arms and legs spread-eagled. I had never seen a live burn case. All the burned soldiers I had seen were dead. We called them "crispy-critters." The man across from me was a gruesome mass of blackened, crusted flesh with a perpetual grimace where his lips had been burned away. There was a constant activity around him as the medical staff fought to keep him alive. Different intravenous tubes, a respirator, the suction machine, and other things were to no avail. The soldier died within a day of my arrival at the ward.

Another burn case was brought in whose whole body was blackened. His skin was curled up in sheets that reminded me of old paint peeling off a ceiling.

He could talk, so I asked him what the hell had happened to him.

"I was burning shit," he answered.

"Burning shit?" I was astounded. Men in a combat zone got shot, blown up, or crushed in machinery while in the service of their country—but "burning shit"? This was a serious blow to my notion of a proper war injury.

Burning shit was a method the American Army used for sanitation purposes. A fifty-five-gallon barrel would be cut off about one-third of the way up from the bottom. This made a large pan that fit under the outdoor privies used at the base camps. The pans would be half filled with diesel fuel, which would soak into the shit. When the pans were about full, they were removed and the shit was burned to dispose of it.

The shit-burner was a gregarious kid who smiled a lot. In fact, his teeth and eyes shining through that dusky burned skin looked exactly like the cat in *Alice in Wonderland*. He didn't mind explaining what had happened.

"Yeah, I had fucked up, so the first sergeant put me on the shit-burning detail. Me and a couple of the other guys were dragging the shit cans over to the fire, when I picked up a can and threw it on the fire, it flashed back on me. Somebody must have put gasoline instead of diesel fuel into the can by mistake. I look like hell but the doctors tell me I won't have any permanent damage. This skin that's peeling off will grow back 'cause they aren't deep burns." He kept on grinning.

We who were in a combat outfit came to believe we were the best and everyone else was just not quite as good. Especially the REAs (Rear Echelon Assholes) in the safe areas. In my drugged mind, I was thinking that noncombat injuries should be in a separate ward by themselves. I believed that men from a combat unit were special. That anchor held me steady against a stream of pain and anxiety about life as an invalid.

But there was a shit-burner right across the aisle from me. Everything in my world was changing. The anchor was slipping.

The soldier to my left, an infantry lieutenant, had shrapnel wounds over most of his body. He had not lost any limbs, but the wounds had pierced many of his internal organs, including his lungs, and he was in constant misery. Of all of us, he complained the most. It was embarrassing to have a fellow second lieutenant complain so much and so loudly. Officers were supposed to set an example for the enlisted men. We were taught to believe that, and it made sense to me. Those lessons taught to us would drift among my thoughts, directing them, helping me get through this thing

I had been thrust into at 0745 hours on 11 January 1968.

Being an officer had nothing to do with it. The fact was that each wounded man needed something to hold onto, something solid and familiar. My recent life as an officer combat leader was my straw to grasp. Therefore, that lieutenant's complaining upset me because it was threatening my beliefs.

I could see only the outline of his head and shoulders because his bed was higher than my cot and was perpendicular to mine. His head would roll back and forth across the pillow as he groaned and cried out. Although he seemed not to know where he was and was probably not conscious of his behavior, I wished he would die or shut up.

Once, toward the end of a four-hour pain shot, all of my hatred toward him rolled out of my mouth.

"For God's sake, Lieutenant! Why don't you shut the fuck up? When you leave here you'll still have everything. You don't have anything to bitch about!"

Perhaps I was feeling sorry for myself, but I felt ashamed and good at the same time for saying it.

Even so, he never heard me and he never did quiet down the whole time I was in that ward.

I automatically categorized wounds as worse or better than mine. It was a way to pass the time as well as fight the pity lingering around the fringes of my thought patterns. Sometimes I couldn't distinguish whether the pity was for myself or for the others.

The ward was pathetic and on bad days when the enemy struck somewhere it got worse as the wounded were flown in. The smell of fresh dirt always accompanied the newly wounded. If a man was brought through the doors of our Quonset hut we knew the wound was serious and we would crane our necks around as he was rolled in. We asked questions of each other and the medical staff to find out who he was: Is he a friend? What unit is he from? What kind of attack was it? How did he get hit? When was he brought in? Where was he? What kind of wound does he have?

Yes, what kind of wound was it—we all wanted to know. No other question ever asked by a soldier is so full of dread.

By the answer we would know the man's future.

Shrapnel and bullets shatter bones, sever nerves, mangle internal organs, amputate limbs, strip faces, eradicate sight, abolish hearing, stifle speech, pulverize sex organs, and ravage minds.

Aircraft, tanks, armored personnel carriers, and utility vehicles blow up, wreck, or crash, causing men to be burned or crushed.

Explosions stun.

Almost every example in various degrees was represented in the hut during my eleven-day stay. We talked of this among ourselves. But I remember two who did not talk.

A soldier at the end of the hut nearest the operating rooms lay immobile; his eyes were bandaged with a wide strip of white gauze wrapped around his head. A tuft of hair stuck up out of the top of the bandage; his lips and lower jaw showed beneath. The middle of his head and face was covered by the white gauze. He never said anything, and he only shifted his body when a nurse or orderly asked him to move when changing the bed sheets. Most blinded soldiers talked a lot. This guy never said anything.

Lying in the bed catty-corner across to my left was a great hulk of a man. When the bandages were removed for debriding of his wounds he looked as if a large ice cream scoop had taken a full dip from his head. I was amazed how much of the head and brain could be removed and the man still be alive. His head reminded me of a basketball caved in on one side when the air has gone out of it. He was little trouble for the ward staff. He would lie quietly on his cot, his eyes perpetually closed in an expressionless face. He showed no response to any stimuli other than turning his face like a heliotrope plant toward the nurses' station when the bright lamp was turned on. I heard a nurse say he would be a vegetable the rest of his life.

The blind soldier had emotions but suppressed everything, and the soldier with half a brain had no emotions at all. However, the rest of us acted emotionally in line with our basic character. At least, whenever we were in control we did.

But the drugs sometimes loosened our controls, causing us to respond to the pain and bizarre surroundings with the survival reactions of animal instinct—such as the first time the surgeon told me he might have to amputate my remaining arm.

Turning Points

"Lieutenant Downs, this is Colonel Ellis. He's going to operate on your arm."

I looked up at a big man dressed in a surgeon's gown. He had a close haircut and looked all business. He also was the oldest doctor I had seen around the wards. He must have been in his fifties.

"Hi, Colonel."

"Hello, Lieutenant. I'm going to look at your arm after we get you ready for surgery and see how it's coming along." He touched the tips of three of my fingers, which were all that could be seen beyond the ridiculously (to me) large bandage around my arm and hand.

"Can you feel that?"

"No."

"How about this?"

"No, no."

"Uhmn. Can you feel this?"

"Not yet—uh, ye—er, no—I'm not sure; what's the matter, Doc?"

"Well, I won't know until I unwrap that arm and hand; but you have nerve damage for sure, and I must tell you so you can be prepared. . . . If your arm has become infected, I may have to amputate it."

The juggernaut of his words rolled through my body. My mind froze, drenched in an icy despair. I stared unbelievingly at him.

"What do you mean, Doc? I'm safe. My arm's still there. I can't lose it now! It's the only one I have left. Look! It's been days since I was hit. It's still there!"

It was incomprehensible to me that American medical techniques could not save my arm. I had always thought doctors were closest to God. The only reason the doctors had not sewed my left arm back on, I believed, was because it was too badly mangled. But here was my right arm still on and this doctor was telling me that medicine is not as powerful as I had always believed. Enough of my beliefs had been destroyed already. I lost control.

"You motherfucker!"

"What?"

"You motherfucker. If you cut off my arm I'll kill you. You dirty motherfucker. Nurse, don't let him do it, you hear? Don't let him do it." I was not yelling. I was making these statements in a matter-of-fact voice. I was full of pain-killing drugs and it seemed to me that I could order my platoon in to protect me. I would have my men kill him. I would kill him. I was so helpless I think I must have gone insane.

I became two entities. I was a rocket orbiting the earth. Red and white barber stripes were my markings and I saw myself in the ward far below. I directed myself downward in a dive toward the earth and the ward where I was. As I dived, an eerie scream sounded from me to let those on earth know I was coming to destroy them all.

I dived through the intensive care ward crashing the wall, ripping through the doctor, causing him to explode all over the ward. I lay in my cot and took joy in his destruction. Then I crashed through the opposite wall and climbed back up into orbit. There I screamed and circled to earth once again to destroy the ward and all that was in it. From my cot I applauded as I crashed through the ward again and again until nothing was left. I exhilarated in the death, the blood, and the destruction.

I orbited while they rolled me into the surgery room. I would kill them all! I was frantic with fear and helplessness. I had no friends here. These people were all strangers. There was no one to speak for me and protect me during my vulnerability.

As they prepared to put me under, the colonel stepped next to me, his mask and rubber gloves on. I concentrated on regaining control of my fear. The logical part of my mind knew the colonel was trying his best to help me. He was going to save my arm, if he could. I knew he was the best shot I had. I forced my will to gain control, to concentrate on what I could identify.

I looked around. The operating room was the Quonset hut next to my ward. The rooms were divided by little cubicles with walls a bit taller than the colonel. There was a nurse and another orderly with us. It was important to me to know where I was. Among all these strangers I needed something to hold on to. As crummy as my ward was, it was at least something I knew. Here in this cubicle I was the stranger, not these people. This was their environment—the place of "near death." If a part of me was dying I should show I was a man.

"Hey, Doc. I'm sorry. But there's been a lot of pain around lately, and you tell me you are going to cut off my arm! It's a lick on me, okay?"

"Sure Lieutenant, I go through it all the time. I don't

.me you. I'll do my job but you have to do yours. A lot of people are depending on you."

I went under with that thought. I was leading my platoon in a fire fight attacking a machine gun nest when I realized the men could no longer hear me. The battle scene faded to be replaced by a room. I was looking up at a familiar orderly.

"Glad to see you back, Lieutenant," he said, smiling. "New bandage and all." I looked at my arm and relief swept over me. It was still there. And so it went. Each day Colonel Ellis would operate. Each day, struggling out of the fog, my first fully conscious act would be to look down for the arm. I dreaded this. Being taken away for an operation every day, I lost control over the decision that would affect my life. It was the only decision that mattered—would they cut off my other arm?

One day as I lay stomach-down in my canvas cot watching my dancing rock spiders maneuver in their infinite patterns, a mop was thrust into my dance group scattering spiders in all directions. I turned my head. Who was screwing up my fantasy world?

I looked right into the eyes of a Vietnamese. He was an old man, with a face eroded by wrinkles, betel-nut-stained teeth and gums, and a whispy white beard dripping from his chin. He was stooped over so he could mop the floor under my cot and he had stopped his mopping when I turned to look at him. He looked back at me for a moment, frozen in his movement as I stared incredulously at him.

What was a Vietnamese doing in an American hospital ward? My confused mind could not separate this old man from the civilians in Quang Ngai province. They had been the enemy. Because of them my platoon's existence had always been tenuous.

Quang Ngai was a ruthless province whose people had never bowed to the South Vietnamese Government. Land mines, booby traps, sniper fire, night attacks, ambushes—all took their toll on my platoon. The people who supplied the Vietcong hated us with a fanatical zeal. We hated them with equal fervor.

I had learned that my life depended on regarding all Vietnamese with a great deal of suspicion. We used to laughingly say, "the only good dink is a dead dink!" Now here was a dink only a few feet from me and I was totally helpless.

"Nurse! There's a dink in here! Get him away," I frantically called over to the nurse's desk, turning quickly back to the old man.

"Get away from me, you dink motherfucker," I said venomously through clenched teeth to the old man. I hated him; I hated and feared him. He was the enemy. So much violence and death over the last five months had seeped deep into my psyche. The drugs in me let everything surface easily.

The old man backed hastily away from my hate, bumping into an old woman whom I noticed for the first time. She was more stooped and older looking than he was. The only other difference was that she didn't have a beard. They both wore the black pajamas indigenous to the population of Vietnam and, unfortunately for the peasants and the Americans, the uniform of the Vietcong.

"Jesus Christ, there's a platoon of dinks in here!" I could barely move my stump, but I waved it slowly pointing at the two Vietnamese who kept backing away from the crazy American.

"Lieutenant Downs! What are you doing? It's okay. This man and his wife are on contract to clean the ward every day. See their badges? They have been cleared!"

"It makes no difference! I killed dinks in the field who had passes on them and grenades and weapons anyway. You don't understand them like I do!" I growled my warning keeping my eyes on the Vietnamese the whole while. The old man held his mop like a shield in front of him to ward off the evil I was projecting.

The nurse called loudly for a doctor. The infantryman on one side of me—opposite the shrapnel-lieutenant—had had his leg blown off and was yelling encouragement. We were both doped up, fresh from combat, and full of turbulent emotions.

The doctor arrived at a trot and gave me a shot to calm me down, but I fought it off because of the danger from the Vietnamese. They finally moved the Vietnamese couple to the other end of the ward and I drifted off to sleep—but only after getting an assurance from the legless infantryman that he would wake me if they came back.

The next day, more lucid, I apologized to the nurses. But I never trusted the Vietnamese and I watched them every time they came into the ward with the mop and bucket.

In a few days I was moved from the center of the ward down to one end. That was where I discovered that enemy soldiers were there in the intensive care ward with us.

"What the hell is going on?" I asked the soldier next to me, who had been paralyzed by a bullet wound in the spine. "That looks like two dinks right across from us."

"That's right, Lieutenant. They put these fucking gooks right in here with us Americans."

Another guy nearby who had both legs gone was in a cot right next to one of the enemy. "You think you got it bad," he told us. "I have to lay next to the bastards. They stink like dinks too. Even in here."

As time went on, I learned a bit more about the two dinks. One of them was a Chinese sniper, seventy-seven years old, who had been shot in the chest three times by an antisniper team. The other was a Vietcong woman who had been shot in the stomach during a night attack on the perimeter. She had massive internal infection and was delirious most of the time.

We all agreed that it was a waste of time to take wounded soldiers as prisoners. All of us compared notes and found that none of our units had taken any prisoners unless we were ordered to. The enemy took no prisoners: We retaliated. Even the idea of bringing in a wounded prisoner instead of just zapping him was ridiculous to us. These two were lucky to be captured back here near a big base camp instead of out in the "bush."

The truth is, we took great glee in the suffering of those two enemy soldiers. We had to give the old Chinese credit though; he tried to be inscrutable through all the pain. But, oh, how he hated the suction machine. With those three chest wounds his upper diaphragm had to be sucked out every couple of hours. When he saw the nurse coming he would look at her with pure hate. She would talk and try to calm him, but she usually had such trouble getting the tube into his side an orderly would have to hold him down. After the machine started, he would start coughing and his face would contort with agony.

We loved it.

Two nights later, after midnight, the American next to the Vietcong woman with the stomach wound hoarsely cried to us, "Wake up!" The word went around our end of the ward; she was dying.

Like dismembered ghouls we lay in the gloom watching the urgent efforts of doctors, nurses, and orderlies as they struggled to save the Vietcong's life. To the medical staff this woman was no enemy. She was a human body brought to them for healing.

But we infantry were different. Our past year's training and recent life of combat had revolved around killing. I had been doing that job of killing, destroying, and surviving quite well. How could I stop now? Why should I stop?

I wanted revenge. I wanted one more crack at killing them. Every man in that ward wanted one more crack.

Part of our revenge came from the Vietcong dink woman, watching her die, anticipating the death, savoring each moment of her pain as she thrashed about beneath the doctor's shadow cast against the curved Quonset wall.

When she died I grunted approval.

"Hey, the bitch is dead!"

"All right! The Vietcong cunt has fucking run out of luck!"

"Serves the fucking gook right. Probably killed her share of Americans with her motherfucking booby traps!"

Smiling grimly at each other, we congratulated ourselves on a job well done. Another dink was added to the body count.

Success? It seemed I measured success in death. Why? Why was I preoccupied with death? True, I had myself been plunged into the well of death when my heart quit beating as I lay on the operating table. But that was not enough to explain it. Relatively few men in any war actually see combat. Those few men who do fight and survive are then in a class by themselves.

To survive they must build a wall, a wall to protect the intellect from death. An infantryman kills other people. He rips life from them any way he can. He sees the lives of his friends and fellow soldiers ripped from them in hideous forms day after day. Often he must order other soldiers to do things that cause them to die or be wounded and those burdens must be shouldered in the mind: the nagging guilt from causing your men's deaths or wounds. When death is too intimate, life becomes a stranger.

Perhaps what I had gone through and was going through was a strengthening of the wall. Or perhaps too much of me had gone into the wall. What part of me had been destroyed?

* * *

A day after the woman died, I took a turn for the worse. Infection somewhere in my body caused a high fever and I became semiconscious. I was moved back to my old position across from the nurse's desk. Colonel Ellis still operated on me about every other day. I alternated between deep depression when he arrived and soaring spirits when I came out of the anesthesia and rediscovered my arm.

I kept dark thoughts to myself and tried to be a good patient, because somewhere during the two weeks since the explosion I had made up my mind that I was going to learn to cope with one arm. I made myself accept the fact that no matter whether I complained, cursed, cried, prayed, hoped for a surgical transplant, wished it hadn't happened, felt self-pity, or waited for a miracle, nothing was going to change the fact that my arm was gone forever. Another arm would not grow back.

As a matter of curiosity I had earlier asked what they did with the severed limbs and other body parts. I remembered the nurse dropping my bloody arm into the plastic sack held by the orderly and I wondered what had happened to it.

The answer was that the limbs were refrigerated for approximately forty-eight hours until it was determined that the patient would live. If he lived, the limb was disposed of in a way determined by the religion stamped onto his dog tags. If he was Catholic or Jewish, the limb was buried. If he was Protestant, the limb was cremated.

If the soldier died within forty-eight hours the limb was embalmed along with the rest of the body and put into an aluminum casket for shipment back to the United States where all of the remains were then sent to the family for burial.

I ruefully thought of my arm being cremated and the ashes spread over Vietnam. I was reminded of the beginning of a poem by the World War I poet Rupert Brooke:

If I should die, think only this of me:
That there's some corner of a foreign field
That is forever England.

A wistful memory of Grandma Downs's Indiana farm made me realize that from now on I was part of two countries. One composed of my birth and love, one of my death and hate.

America and Vietnam were the poles of raging emotion in me. Having ridden my fury to destruction, I was left behind as flotsam from the storm. Whether I became a derelict or not would depend on me. I had a choice. Either I went through life feeling sorry for myself and generally making myself and everyone around me miserable or I overcame this disaster by being positive. I liked people, I loved life, I enjoyed being happy, I liked to do things. One day I could no longer tolerate lying in a bed.

It had been two weeks, and I was bored, forced to lie quiet all of the time. I couldn't move into a comfortable position; all positions had some pain. I couldn't read because there was no way to hold a book. The busy staff had time only for short conversation, and the men around me were in too much pain or too drugged for much talk.

So, I told the nurses that I would like to try to walk. Nobody believed I was serious. But I kept at them, cajoling. They knew how mutilated I was from the waist down, and they didn't think I would be able to stand up, much less take a step. But I finally convinced them that I could try. If they didn't help me I threatened to sing "The Blue-Tail Fly" again.

I was thrilled now at the prospect of getting out of bed and actually walking. I could see myself moving about pretty well within a few days. There would be some pain, but I could handle it.

The nurses, orderlies, and wounded men watched with

anticipation as two orderlies prepared to help me up. The sheet was removed from my naked body. They put their hands under my shoulders and gently lifted.

As they did I cried out involuntarily in surprise and fear as horrible pain tore through my buttocks and legs. "Wait! Oh, God, that hurts! Oh, my God." Sweat, cold chills, and muscle spasms overcame me.

As the orderlies held my shoulders partly off the cot, I realized that I had made a drastic error. I had not moved in two weeks. Now, fire raced along my nerves. Dozens of wire stitches were strung across my wounds to keep them from tearing open farther. I had disturbed those torn muscles and tendons that the stitches held and I had put weight on my buttocks.

The waves of pain were so intense that they swept the damping effects of the pain killer away. I gritted my teeth against the pain. Everyone was watching me. I could not let them down, or myself.

"It's a lick, but I'm infantry. Move me slowly on up." I gasped out with a bravado I did not feel. My face crinkled from the pain.

Why was I always getting myself into things like this, I thought. Jesus H. Christ, this hurts. I could feel the tears running down my cheeks.

After a lot of exertion by the orderlies, encouragement by onlookers and determination to succeed on my part, I was finally being held in a sitting position, slumped on the edge of the cot, my legs hanging down. For the first time in days I looked around me from a vertical position. But to sit on the wounds was so painful that I told the orderlies to lift me out onto the floor. They picked me up under my armpits and lowered me, put slippers on my feet, and slipped a robe around my shoulders, holding me all the while. I simply could not stand by myself.

When my full weight was taken upon my legs the effect

on my body was more excruciating pain, dizziness, and a tremendous urge to throw up. If there had been anything in my stomach I would have lost it. My body shivered from cold, exertion, pain, and nausea.

Bent at the knees and waist, I could not straighten up. There was just too much damage, too many wire stitches, and too much pain. I crouched like an old man as the two orderlies held me under the armpits. Slowly I slid a foot forward a few inches. My first step!

Everyone who had two hands applauded and the others shouted encouragement. God! It was a happy moment. Achievement! Success was a heady feeling. The accolades I received were like extra energy to me.

"Number Fucking One, Lieutenant," one of the men hollered from his bed.

Buoyed by my success I shuffled partway down the aisle with the help of the two orderlies who supported most of my weight. In front of the nurse's desk, they sat me gently on a chair prepared by the nurses, padded with two pillows. Even with two pillows the nerve ends in my buttocks screamed for relief. I sat slumped over. I asked for something to read and an orderly handed me a comic book about war. I tried to read a page about a German soldier but I was unable to concentrate because of the pain, nausea, and vertigo.

After a few minutes I needed to be put back into my cot. The enormity of the terrible damage to my body had a sobering effect on me and, although I put up a cheerful front, I was very worried about my future as a functioning human being. In the movies the wounded moved and talked with hardly any trouble at all. But this pain—my missing arm, my legs—my God but it was going to be a long time until I was well again. "Those fucking movies I saw never told the whole story and, even if they did, would I have realized what I was seeing?"

Waves of nausea and dizziness swept through me as the

orderlies lifted me back into my cot. I became incoherent
for short periods of time. My mind seemed to short out,
overloaded like an electrical wire struck by lightning during
a windstorm.

The nurses worried over me all night. I did not attempt
to get out of bed again soon.

Passing the Time

Wounded soldiers moved constantly in and out of the
ward. As a man improved he would go to the regular ward
in the Quonset hut next door to make room for the stream
of casualties arriving from the field.

Since there wasn't anything else to do except study our
closed environment, we quickly became attuned to the details that affected our lives. For instance, if a bed was placed
in front of the nurse's station, as mine was, that soldier was
in bad shape and had to be kept close, where the nurses could
keep an eye on him. The beds on the ends contained the less
critical intensive care cases, and if a patient was moved out
to another Quonset hut he had passed from immediate danger. I had been in the intensive care ward next to the nurse's
station for about two weeks. If the others were being moved
next door and I wasn't, something was awry. I worried about
that a lot. "What exactly was wrong with me?" I thought.

Of course, there were the men who were moved out because they died. Today, that Quonset hut looms darkly in
my memory. When death entered our ward I sensed the thin
fabric of life quiver, stretched tautly as a spider's web from
man to man. We lay helplessly ensnarled as death purpose-
fully moved among us to pick a life force to suck into ob-
literation.

When the men you are among prepare to die, your
thoughts race crazily around and around inside your skull

like motorcycles at a county fair, speeding around the inside walls of a large barrel. The centrifugal force keeps the riders from falling onto the floor below. The faster the bikes go the tighter they cling to the wall. My speeding thoughts were my reassurance I would not fall. Death would take the weaker or unsuspecting ones first.

It wasn't that I was afraid of death, but that I was falling in love with living. I had finally noticed life, like the girl next door who had always been there. I was beginning to appreciate her finer qualities.

I believe some men died that should not have because they lost interest in experiencing life again.

The month of January 1968 recorded a lot of casualties as the flow of wounded poured into the hospitals.

I had been wounded on the eleventh of January in a heavily congested area in which our company had been fighting for a week. No one had to tell us soldiers that the dinks were planning something big because the dinks had more ammunition and weapons than usual. They engaged us more readily. Their tactics had always been hit and run, especially down in the flat ground. They had always chosen the place of battle very carefully and made us search for them, to coax them into battle.

But the operations we went on after the Christmas truce in 1967 were different. Now the dinks fought more pitched battles. They had ample mortar shells, high explosives, land mines, and rifle ammunition.

That was fine with us. We wanted them to stand and fight. Although casualties were higher on both sides, we could always come out ahead because we had superior firepower and we could kick their asses. Those of us in the field didn't know that January would go down in the history books as the beginning of the big Tet offensive of 1968. I would go down in history as only a number representing one of the early casualties of that event, as would most of my platoon.

One day I was shocked when one of the men from my platoon was moved into the bed catty-cornered from me. It was Gary, a rifleman. Both of his legs had been blown off above the knees. The last time I had seen Gary he had been a strapping man capable of humping the boonies all day long, and steady as a rock. He was an easygoing man from my home state, Indiana. I was sick at heart to see him lying there with no legs.

I felt disoriented. I had wanted my platoon back and now here was one of the men from my platoon but he had had his legs blown off.

"Hey, Sir! Delta 1–6! We're back together! It's good to see you! The guys miss you. The platoon wasn't the same after you left."

I smiled bravely. "Hey! Heyyy! Don't you worry. They take good care of you here. But what happened for Christ's sake?"

"It was a lick sir. They assigned a dog team to us about a week after you got hit and on an operation the dog sniffed out a dink who was captured. The dink told an interpreter that he would lead us to an arms cache. None of us trusted the dink and we didn't want to let him sucker us into a trap, but we had to give it a try. Shit! We were set up good.

"I was with the point squad that day and Vince was behind me. As we approached a hedgerow the dink started trotting ahead of us and ran through an opening in the hedgerow."

"Goddamn, wasn't the dink tied up? You can't trust those fucking dinks. I would have killed him. None of that prisoner bullshit for me."

"Yeah. That's what the guys were saying. You wouldn't have let that dink live long enough to talk about an arms cache. Anyway I started after him and stepped on a Bouncing Betty which blew my legs off. A piece of shrapnel hit Vince's LAW (light anti-tank weapon) which he was carrying slung across his chest. The rocket exploded and blew him right in half. It was a fucking lick; six guys got it. I hated that area." He paused in a moment of introspection. "I don't know why, but the dinks are getting so they fight more."

"That's no shit. I don't know how long I've been here but it seems like there are a lot more wounded coming in."

We talked on, both of us drifting in and out of pain and drugs.

Gary's presence helped me realize how much my mind freely flowed under the effect of drugs. We rambled on to each other during our individual brief spurts of clarity and, if we both happened to be coherent at the same time, our conversation centered on our routine experiences with the platoon—Delta 1–6—and the men. This was the rock we grasped.

But during the periods after the pain-killing shots, I didn't care about the people around me. I became an impartial observer to all around me.

Gary became a distant figure too far away to hear what I was saying although he seemed to desperately want to reply.

During lucid moments I felt a warning disquiet about my reluctance to relate to someone I knew. Up to now I had accepted my isolation because I knew none of the people in the wards. My reaction to Gary made me think that perhaps my isolation stemmed from a natural protective mechanism. My physical prowess was nonexistent; consequently, only will power stood between me and defeat. Defiance against my assault was a fury that threatened to overwhelm me, but I always persevered. Life, however tenuous and painful, was preferable to death.

But I was beginning to worry it would be a Pyrrhic victory if the struggle cost me my psychological well-being. I didn't want to become an embittered old man over this. Goddamn, something else to worry about.

Not being able to do anything for hours and days on end was nearly as hard to bear as the pain. I couldn't use my hands to hold a book or turn its pages, couldn't write, could hardly move, and couldn't carry on lengthy conversations because either I or the men on the beds next to me were shot full of drugs or too full of pain to concentrate; there also was no radio, no television—nothing! The only thing working was the brain and, when it wasn't out on a drug trip or contemplating my future, I relieved my boredom somewhat by studying the activities around me.

Most pleasurable were the times when someone focused directly on me, even if it was a doctor or a nurse come to cause pain by working on the wounds; at least, it was somebody to talk with, someone to help slip a few minutes by.

My goal had been to recover in a year, but that year was sure dragging by. Every minute gone was good riddance.

The doctors, nurses, and orderlies did what they could. In their off hours, their only relief from our misery, many of them dropped around to check on us, to help write a letter, or just to talk for a few minutes. They were our only family. Care of patients was their life.

There was a leper colony outside Qui Nhon which some of the medical staff visited on a regular basis after working their regular twelve-hour shift. The enemy reportedly never harmed them although they went in unarmed jeeps.

The medical staff was our first step in beginning to adjust. Part of the ward routine were rounds conducted by those who helped us do the things we couldn't do for ourselves. Our personal belongings, everything from our pockets when we were wounded, were set now in brightly colored cloth tote bags tied to the end of our cots. Red Cross ladies would fish into the bags for things we wanted—pictures, old letters.

They would also write letters home for those who couldn't write.

The physical therapist came once a day, drilling me on how to move my stump in circles so the muscles wouldn't atrophy. That it seemed a waste of time was beside the point. She said she wanted me to start thinking about using that stump instead of considering it as a thing that would hang there the rest of my life. She brought me pictures of men with both arms gone. They were shown with prosthetic devices, doing everything from fly casting to driving a car. When I got back to the States, she said, I would be fitted with a prosthesis right away. I would be surprised at how agile I'd be. At an amputee program at Denver, Colorado, men with one leg missing were learning to ski.

"Yeah, fine," I thought. "But what would my family and friends think of me with no arm. What would my wife think? Or my daughter?"

One day the therapist taped a pen to the bandage covering my hand and made me write a letter home. I was able to scratch out only a few shaky lines, but my morale and confidence soared from that small achievement.

This woman was typical of the occupational and physical therapists I would meet in the months to come. Eternal optimists, they would cajole, threaten, force, kid, and humor us to bend that finger or arm, put the round peg in the round hole, draw, and write, but, most of all, to keep the mind busy and make us prove to ourselves that we could if we only tried and never, never gave up.

There was also the chaplain. He cruised by every day to say something cheerful and then moved on. He never did anything for my spirits. I felt it was just a job with him and the quicker he could get out of the ward the better he liked it. What faith I'd had in the "Man of Peace," Jesus Christ, was gone, blown away with my arm. My problem with God was only a part of the disillusionment I had with the many beliefs I carried from childhood. The devastating effect the war had had on my naiveté only grew in the hospital.

A nighttime Vietcong attack didn't help. It was only a perimeter raid, but men from the other wards who weren't seriously wounded were rushed out on the line. Those of us in intensive care were put on litters on the floor next to the bed or under it. Extra blankets and pillows protected us if a mortar shell came through the roof, or a satchel charge was thrown through the door, or an RPG (rocket-propelled grenade) was fired in to the wall. The blankets dismayed and terrified us. They would not stop shrapnel. In the gloom of the darkened ward, the sound of battle on the perimeter rammed toward us. In our drugged minds we vividly imagined a Vietcong opening the door at the end of the ward and running down the aisle firing his AK-47 into our defenseless bodies. The dinks would do this. Shooting up a hospital ward would mean nothing to them.

We cried out to the orderlies to get us some weapons, M-16s. The men with good arms could protect the rest of us. The orderlies ignored us, of course.

Finally the attack subsided and we were lifted back into our beds. But a change had come over the ward. We were psyched up, back in the war. Dim lights and shadows turned to jungle, a backdrop for me and my platoon. Even Yoder was there, dead though he was, killed in an ambush just before Thanksgiving 1967.

I was the last man to talk to Yoder before the Chinese Communist machine gun splattered his life away against a jungle mountainside. A boy from Knoxville, Tennessee, who died young on a mountain in South Vietnam.

He had joined the army, he said, because he had no future anywhere else.

"Hey! Yoder! It's a lick on you! There's no future at all for you now!" I hollered good naturedly at him where he was standing among the shadows between the wounded men across from me. His missing front tooth made his raw-boned features more hillbilly looking than usual. His pack hung from his back, crossed bandoliers of ammo were layered over his chest, and an M-16 was held loosely in his right hand.

He smiled back. "Fucking A, sir."

The strangest aspect of these fantasies was the total realism of the people and the situation. Whether I was talking to a dead man or flying through the air as a destructive missile, they all were as true as the floor, the ceiling, my cot, and my pain.

I rarely fought it. In fact, I preferred the fantasy world and, although I could force myself out of it, I seldom did, at least not at first. Later, as I healed, fantasy fell away, losing its sharpness and clarity. That night was the last night Yoder ever visited me with such definition.

One day without warning, I was moved to the ward next door. This was a mixed blessing. It was all a part of the healing and a sure sign that I was better, but each time I was moved for any reason the staff had to redetermine my blood type. This was done as routinely for a move of three bed spaces as for a journey of a thousand miles. It had to be. Each ward staff was responsible for every patient and a pint of the wrong blood could kill you.

Dozens of needles had been stuck into the few available places on my body. My blood vessels were now so tough that it was difficult to find a place in which to stick a needle. Working down my body, therefore, they had come finally to the veins on top of my feet.

I hated that. It was one of the few places that didn't hurt.

To compound the agony, I knew what would happen after they completed their test. My blood was A negative, but from the beginning they had been using O negative because it is the universal donor. I had lost most of my own blood and there was just too little A negative to go around. So the blood test would show a mixture of two types, mine and the blood I had been given. The tester was sure to call for another sample.

Nothing changed that routine; no amount of information I rationally delivered to an orderly could make him stop probing. Orderlies had heard so many stories from doped-up patients that they just nodded condescendingly and continued to poke away at the top of my feet. When at last the confusion cleared and blood flowed into me, I grew cold and would shiver for the hour or so it took to empty the plastic bag. Blood was always stored in a freezer until just before it was to be used. It was precious cargo, all the way from "The World."

As I lay there in misery, shivering, I looked at the other beds full of wounded and reflected on the grotesque premeditation of our wounding. It is better to wound an enemy soldier than to kill him. This ward was a graphic example: A dead soldier requires very little from his country—shipment back home, burial. But a wounded soldier requires a great deal. A large part of the budget for the military must be set aside for expensive equipment, hospitals, medical staff, support personnel, medicine—the list goes on and on. Medical care can drag on for years. Psychological care can last a lifetime.

Countries deliberately develop many types of weapons that are designed to maim a soldier instead of kill him.

As the cold blood dripped steadily through the tubes into my veins, I remembered our training classes on the doctrine of land warfare and weapons.

It was one thing to talk about a land mine and have the instructor describe how it would maim a man's body and another thing to lay in a cot ruefully reflecting on that lesson.

* * *

John Bell, one of the black enlisted men in my platoon, visited me after I was moved into the new ward. He had been injured when Hunter, my pointman, had stepped on a booby trap a few days before I was wounded. We had put both men on a dust-off but had wondered how badly they had been hurt.

John was able to ambulate and was in good spirits. This was the second time he had been wounded, so according to battalion policy he would not have to return to the field.

John had been wounded the day Yoder was killed. We had a lot to talk about and the visit was good for my morale. He told me the platoon had asked him to give them a report on my condition. I told him to say, "It was a lick on me!"

I got a treat one day when my company executive officer (XO), Lieutenant Smart, stopped by to visit. I had taken over his platoon when I arrived in Delta Company so we had a lot in common. We talked quietly for a while and when he rose to leave he asked me about the platoon's beer money that I had been carrying. About ninety dollars U.S., I told him, and that it ought to be in my wallet in the little bag at the end of my bed. He checked but discovered that all of my money had been stolen. We agreed on the multitude of assholes in the world who would steal from a wounded man.

While we discussed the theft, I started to feel very sick. Large red bumps popped out all over the left side of my body. Lieutenant Smart called quickly to a nurse who, when she saw what was happening, yelled for help. I had been hooked up to a unit of bad blood. She yanked the intravenous tube out of my body and called for a doctor, working quickly but efficiently on me as I started to lose consciousness. Before I faded I said goodbye to Lieutenant Smart and told him to tell Delta 6 and the men that I was doing okay. Then I lost consciousness.

* * *

I was coming along and in a few days I was well enough to be moved to Japan, with an overnight stop at Clark Air Force Base in the Philippines. There were just too many wounded coming in to keep me any longer.

A rumor was going around the ward about a booby trap the Vietcong had hidden on the door to the outside latrine between the two wards used by the medical staff. We discussed this hot topic because stories abounded about men who were wounded on their last day in Vietnam. We all agreed it would be double jeopardy if we were wounded again.

I sure was ready to leave Vietnam.

I was loaded on a hospital bus equipped to take tiers of litters on both sides. After a painful ride, we reached the airplane. We were high in morale as they prepared to load us on the plane. It was great to be away from the boredom of the ward.

Two of the wounded going to Japan had been hit when their chopper had flown through a B-52 strike area just as the bombs had gone off under them, blowing them out of the air. The helicopter crew chief had a broken back and was paralyzed but he kept asking for a description of the plane. His pilot, the only other crash survivor, had massive internal injuries but he gave the crew chief a pretty good rundown even so. We were all laughing.

The jerking and stopping of the bus; the orderlies carrying the litters out the back door and laying us on the ground; the waiting and then being picked up to be carried up the ramp into the plane; and the snapping and locking in of the litter to the tier along the fuselage of the aircraft—the excitement of it all caused a bad reaction in me somehow.

I became very nauseated. Everything spun. As my litter was fastened onto the plane, I told the nurse something wasn't right. She worried over me until the plane took off, and then I lost consciousness as we left Vietnam.

CHAPTER 3
Clark Air Force Base
The Philippines
27 January 1968

I came to as they transferred us off the plane, down the ramp to be loaded in tiers on the bus. It was cloudy but not raining and I looked around for the band to welcome us, but there was none. This disappointed me. I had expected something. Perhaps we weren't back in "The World" yet. We would surely be given a great welcome home with a band and speeches when we reached the U.S.

The road to the Clark Air Force Base Hospital was miserably rough. Each bump wrung groans out of the wounded. Finally we arrived at a hospital that looked very American. My room was a double. A twenty-year-old sergeant whose eyes had been gouged out by a booby trap lay in the bed closest to the door. We were, at last, in real beds. There were large glass windows in one wall to my left, a television set on the wall opposite us, and a personal listening device about the size and shape of half a clamshell next to the pillow so the sound of the television would not disturb the other patients.

The sergeant and I introduced ourselves and exchanged the usual series of questions the wounded always asked—shop talk:

"What's your name?" (Name, not rank. Rank didn't mean much at this stage.)

"What unit you with?" (We wanted to know army, marines, brigade, or whatever gave the unit its status. Airborne, river patrol, engineers, etc.)

"What were you?" (Rifleman, door gunner, pointman, medic, helicopter crewman, etc.)

"What area you work in?" (I, II, III, or IV Corps, and usually the name of the closest Vietnamese landmark whether it was a village, highway, or geological area. The three categories everything fell into were the Delta, Coastal, or Central Highlands.)

"What kind of shit you guys get into?" (What was the nature of the enemy? Was he Vietcong or North Vietnamese Army? Were there a lot of booby traps, ambushes, civilians? Was the terrain mountainous, swampy, or paddies?)

"What happened to you?" (How did you get wounded, circumstances leading up to it; what happened during and afterward; what happened to the other men and the unit? Explain all aspects of the wound; when did you get hit?)

"How bad is it?" (No matter how serious the wound—blindness, spinal injury, amputation, or whatever, we all clung to hope that we would get better. The answer always started out "The doctors say we have to wait a little longer before we know for sure . . ." We grasped that simple statement as holy word from God Almighty. To supplement the Word was the next part of the answer—"As soon as I get back to 'The World' . . ." Back in America was where the salvation would be performed. "The World" was the basis for our hope. They could do anything there.)

"How long you been here?"

"When you leaving?"

"What's it like here?" (Details on the staff, other men on the ward, what is this ward; burns, amputations, general, where is this located in the chain of medical care leading back to "The World"?)

After we had gone through the questions, the blind sergeant asked me to describe what was around us.

"Son of a bitch," I thought. "Am I lucky to have lost only an arm. What would I do if I were blind? Probably kill myself!"

I described the room and the view outside the window. Those windows made me nervous. Six months of combat had conditioned me to avoid exposure to sniper fire.

Combat does that to a man. To survive one had to think and react to the environment and the situation. As I write this now, I muse at how I am still prone to be startled at any unexpected sharp noise. Reactions become second nature. To act efficiently without thinking is very important in the bush. In the time it took to analyze a noise, the enemy could kill you.

Outside the window tropical bushes and trees swayed violently in the wind. A storm was blowing up. The sky was dark gray. It had turned gray the morning I stepped on the Bouncing Betty. As far as I could ascertain the sky had remained gray since that morning. I loved sunshine and there was a longing in my heart for it.

Large rain drops splattered against the windows. The late afternoon sky turned black as the front of the storm swept toward the hospital. The palm trees whipped back and forth and lightning cracked in a continual display of jagged bolts and enveloping sizzles of light. I had always loved to be out in the rain and the storms when I was growing up in Indiana, but in the jungle it rained so often that now I only wanted to be dry for a long while.

Watching the rain pouring down outside, being safe here in a clean bed, an American place, filled me with a sense of security. I was in a dry, warm place.

I described the lightning, the wind, everything about the storm to the sergeant. He would never see a storm again and I had never really described one until now. I had lived on the earth but not understood it. Having experienced death I would now experience life.

In our room, away from the violence of the storm, the black and white television set was on. A strikingly beautiful Philippine singer stood clutching a microphone on a small stage. I was describing her to the sergeant when a Catholic chaplain walked in. He introduced himself briskly and without further ado launched into a monologue about our wounds. Basically, it came down to this—we had been wounded because Jesus Christ was crucified on the cross. He had suffered; therefore, we must suffer.

I stared at him in astonishment. Surely there were many reasons for my pain, all of them caused by man. I became angry.

He believed what he was saying and was doing his duty, even trying to help us through. But I was having none of it.

My grandparents raised me to believe in God, the Bible, and a religious way of life. There was much death and pain in the Bible, but as a young boy growing up I didn't attend to what that meant because the stories were related to man and God, neither of which I questioned, merely obeyed. Besides, the stories were two thousand years and older, dating back to the beginning of time. I could not comprehend two thousand years, let alone Creation.

Concerning the matter of God and myself I had come to the conclusion that He was not a better person than I am. He may be a Supreme Being, but I feel I can meet Him as an equal and argue my case some day if I have to. I figured He had as many problems in His way as I did in mine. If He is fair, He will listen to reason.

On the battlefield God obviously was not taking much of an interest in each person. I had come to depend on myself because I was real. God was abstract. The more misery, death, inhumanity, and degradation I saw around me, the more abstract the idea of God became.

With this came a distrust of chaplains. This one reminded me of my disillusionment, causing me more anger. I refused to speak to him, staring at his face the whole time he was in the room.

He fidgeted with his rosary as he nervously completed his preachment, finishing with his hands held together, saying a prayer. His hands shook and his eyes darted from object to object in the room. After his prayer he left quickly.

"Shit," I stated.

We were scheduled to be at Clark for only a day, but it was to be an eventful stay, wrought with virulence and pain.

Two Philippine doctors came in an hour or so after the chaplain and stopped at the sergeant's bed. He asked me what was going on and I told him two Philippine dinks were checking him out. When I asked the two if they could speak English, they ignored me. They couldn't, I surmised.

If this was an American military hospital, why were Filipinos allowed in? I stewed over this question while they stood by the blind sergeant and conferred.

Then they came over to my bed, one on each side. I lay there wondering what was going on as they talked to each other, pointing at and probing me as they talked.

"Hey, cut that out," I said as one pressed too hard against my right arm.

Suddenly they reached a decision and began to unwrap my arm and hand. This had never been done while I was conscious, so I was startled and frantically looked around for an American medical person, someone whom I could trust. But the dinks had shut the door to our room.

"Hey! You guys get the fuck out of here and leave me alone," I said weakly, pulling away from them. They grabbed my arm back, jerking it about painfully, as they brusquely unwrapped the bandages.

The sergeant, now concerned, asked what was going on.

I told him something was wrong and asked him to ring for a nurse quickly. When a nurse came to the door, the doctor on my left stepped over and said something to her; she looked briefly at me and closed the door.

When he returned I looked up at both of them to see total unconcern over my condition on their faces. They were merely curious about my wound from a purely professional standpoint.

I was afraid. They were not Americans and they seemed not to care about me. For the first time since I had been wounded I was back among dinks and helpless. My heart pounded rapidly against my chest as the dinks continued their painful machinations, totally unconcerned by my distress.

The sergeant kept encouraging me as I cried out and groaned from the pain; the fucking dinks were killing me. Talking was like biting down on a stick against the pain so I kept talking and talking to the sergeant.

Each layer of bandage was now blood soaked and each roll of bandage was stuck to the layer under it. The dinks roughly ripped it loose, working their way closer to the wound. The last few layers of bandages were so impregnated with blood that ripping them loose caused black streaks of pain to flash across my consciousness. I was going into shock. I was trapped. I could not escape and no one was protecting me. It was like the night the dinks attacked the perimeter of the 85th Evac. There was nothing I could do except endure.

Finally the last layer came off. Only a fine layer of netlike cloth remained. Blood was seeping out the length of my arm from the elbow down to the fingertips.

I growled like an animal and pushed myself away from the Filipinos but they held my arm and steadily ripped the mesh off the length of my arm. The muscles, tendons, and both bones were bared and glistened moistly as blood welled out over the length of my arm.

I stared in horror, remembering, crazily, my high school biology book with its clear plastic pages in one of the chapters showing overlays of the bones, muscles, tendons, organs, and skin of the human body.

My arm looked like the sheet showing the muscles and tendons.

The doctors moved my fingers. Excruciating pain ran up my arm. The pain of having the net pulled loose from the meshed flesh and coagulated blood caused me to keep passing out, but my deep survival instinct coupled with hatred and resentment forced me back to consciousness.

I thrashed back and forth moaning from the pain and degradation of helplessly lying in the filth of my own blood-encrusted dressings. The two Philippine doctors finally walked out, leaving me bloody, exhausted, much nearer death. Tortured into an insane rage by suffering and defilement I envisioned myself firing an M-60 machine gun into their bodies. I shot out of orbit to destroy them. There was a difference, though. For the first time, I turned on myself. After destroying the doctors, I crashed into myself and exploded into fragments toward infinity. It was as if I experienced the crash from two perspectives—myself as destroyer missile and myself as soldier. As I turned for a final dive I saw through the hospital walls down into my room, down to my body lying in the bed. As a missile I had to increase my speed to the ultimate in the dive so that the crash would be intensified. Speed and noise were power, and power was needed for the destruction I wished. It would take a lot of power to kill me.

As I lay in my bed watching myself approach at an awesome rate of speed I rose up from my bed with a guttural snarl and steeled myself to fight against myself.

When we collided there was a volcanic detonation of

sound, colossal boiling clouds, and a sea of dazzling, sparkling lights, scattering into pieces.

Everything was surrounded with, immersed in, and throbbing with waves of burning, excruciating pain.

I wanted to throw up, but only bile and stomach acid were there.

The sergeant was screaming at me now, asking over and over what was happening. Was I okay? "Fast, I need help fast," I groaned.

I vaguely remember American nurses and doctors doing things to my body but for the first time I hovered in limbo between survival and giving up. The pain was so bad that I just wanted to escape it and the only way out was death.

A terrible thunderstorm raged through part of the night. I concentrated on the lightning as a way of not giving up. Cold blood was given to me intravenously all night. I shivered constantly.

I have little memory of the next day when I was moved with the rest of the wounded to a plane for the trip to Japan. A nurse was by my side during much of the flight. She probably felt I was dying. I didn't care. I had been ill-used. I was almost ready to die and close to deciding I had nothing to live for.

CHAPTER 4

The 249th Evac

Camp Drake outside Tokyo, Japan
28 January–9 February 1968

My condition deteriorated so rapidly that when the plane landed I was loaded on a dust-off that had been waiting to fly me to the hospital. After landing, I was hustled to a ward where I lost consciousness.

I regained consciousness eight hours later in a recovery ward filled with soldiers fresh in from Vietnam. All were in bad shape. A sergeant about twenty-four years old in the cot to my right had been crushed by an M-60 tank. His right leg and arm were gone. I had come back far enough to be curious about him. I asked him what the hell happened.

"Damn, Lieutenant. You never saw such a fuck-up. We had a base camp set up next to this village on Highway 9. There hadn't been much happening except for a few patrols getting ambushed and some land mines being set in the road, so we had it pretty easy.

"Something was going on because the gooks had been more active, but we didn't know what. Then one day they started an attack on one of the bridges down the road on the other side of the village in broad daylight. Shit, they never did that before.

"You know how it is, sir. There was a lot of excitement in the base camp. Mill around mill was S.O.P. (Standard

Operating Procedure) for a while with everyone thinking the gooks were breaching the wire. Finally the word came down that the bridge was being overrun and that volunteers were needed to go help defend it. My lieutenant volunteered us so we commandeered a jeep and took off through the gate on the road through the village.

"The fucking gooks picked that time to hit the village. It was the dry season and the dust from the vehicles running both directions on the road was so thick that we couldn't see a damn thing. We drove through one fire fight near the edge of the village before we knew what was going on. I was driving, so I just floorboarded it and drove like hell. We got through that okay and I had slowed down because of the refugees and the traffic. I never did understand those refugees. Here we were driving down the road to a fire fight at a bridge, we had just driven through a fire fight back at the village, and refugees were on the road going in both directions. Fucked up! That's what those people are. Fucked up.

"Anyway, there was mass confusion and dust everywhere like I told you. The sounds of gunfire were fucking everywhere and I was weaving in and out of refugees and wreckage when all of a sudden this big fucking M-60 tank lumbers through the dust on my side of the road right for me. He must have been running toward the other fight. I swerved to the left but he was going full bore and ran right over the top of our jeep. I lunged to the left, but I was too late. My right leg and arm were crushed in the wreckage of the jeep. The amazing thing was I didn't lose consciousness. The fucking tank ran right over the lieutenant. He didn't have a prayer. And you know what those track assholes did? They kept right on going. Those motherfuckers, those rotten motherfuckers! They must've thought we were gooks!

"I had to be cut out of the jeep. My lieutenant, he never had a chance. Those motherfuckers!"

The sergeant and I talked back and forth for fifteen or

twenty minutes, reviewing the sorriness of all track assholes.

Meanwhile, the difficulty of getting an intravenous tube into me arose again. An orderly, nurse, and the ward master discussed their failure to find a vein for their blood sample and decided to go for my femoral artery. They had to have a doctor do that because of the large nerve that runs close to that major artery. It would be a dangerous procedure.

I vainly protested, telling them that my blood type was A negative but that it wouldn't test out that way because of the O negative I had been receiving.

I cursed my helplessness to get my point across as we waited for the doctor. He arrived, discussed the problem with everyone except me, and prepared to drive a needle through my groin. The needle looked about a foot long.

He warned me not to move as he pushed the needle and it was good to have the warning because it felt like a white-hot lance had been thrust into me. At least I was a little prepared for something, otherwise I would have jumped out of bed. As it was, I just used will power to cope with the pain. I had no other choice. I made myself outlast the pain.

After the doctor had withdrawn the blood and it had been removed for testing, I drifted in and out of consciousness, even when they returned for the second test that I knew was coming.

Finally pain won out. I lost consciousess.

I never saw the sergeant again. I heard later that he had died while he lay next to my unconscious body retelling me the story of the M-60 tank leaving them crushed in the road.

I regained consciousness in a large hundred-bed ward. There was a row of beds on each side and a double row head to head up the middle. The nurse's station was at the end of the ward. I was in the middle row on the side closest to the latrines and about ten beds up from the nurse's station. I guessed from my position that I was still in danger.

The ward was a one-story building connected to other buildings designed in the same manner. The spread-out, interlocking system was a common army design for hospitals throughout the world. The ward had opaque windows along one side and tile floors, and was painted a light green.

It seemed that my body was building up a resistance to the drugs because after a shot now the pain eased for only an hour instead of carrying me through the complete cycle of four hours between shots. My mind was therefore clearer for longer periods of time, and although that time was more pain ridden, it was also more real.

Friends

As a consequence, at the 249th I started to take a more active role in what went on around me. Friendships with the nurses, orderlies, and ward staff took on more depth.

Without the dulling effects of drugs, I began to enjoy living more. I was not in utopia, but I was coming back from the brink of death and any distance I traveled from there accelerated my recovery.

After I had graduated from Fort Benning OCS on 14 February 1967, out of the 92nd Company, I had been assigned to an AIT (Advanced Infantry Training) Company at Fort Gordon, Georgia. The men we trained went on to airborne school after AIT and many of them were assigned to the 82nd, 173rd, and 101st airborne units. I had trained approximately six hundred men during that period.

By a coincidence of time, assignment of the 101st Airborne Unit to I Corps, and the increased enemy activity, I found that the ward held a number of these men. The first knowledge I had of this was within a day after entering the ward. A man was rolling by in a wheelchair checking name tags at the ends of the beds when he spotted mine. We traded the standard questions.

"Lieutenant Downs! Is that you, sir? It's me, Corporal James."

"Hey, it's good to see you. Made corporal, huh? What unit were you with?"

"101st Airborne."

"101st? Hey, that's the unit my outfit, the Third of the Fourth Division, was helping out when I got hit. You guys were in a world of shit up there. Goddamn, we never saw so many dinks. That area was definitely hard-core and those dinks were hard-core. Shiit! It was a lick on us. What happened to you?"

"Would you believe a gook with an AK-47? The fucker popped up out of a spiderhole and sprayed my whole squad. I took five hits in the legs but the dust-off got right in there and lifted us out." He looked down at his legs. "I don't know if I'll be able to walk or not. The doctors are saying I have a lot of nerve damage. . . . But we zapped the motherfucker. The point man hit him in the chest with a full load from his M-16. What happened to you, sir?"

"Would you believe a Bouncing Betty?"

"No shit! You still got your legs?"

"Yeah, but just barely. Fuck, I almost lost my right arm. I'm still worried about that. I'm still not sure I'll be able to walk yet. I tried it once and thought I was going to die. My ass was blown away and is held together with wire stitches. I haven't tried to shit yet and I'm not looking forward to it. Shitting through all those wires holding my asshole together ain't gonna be any fun if everything I've gone through so far is any indication."

James laughed like a banshee. "Goddamn, sir, you are due for a world of hurt! The guy in the bed next to me has the same problem and after the first time of going through that he refuses to eat anything solid!"

"Thanks, James, I feel better already," I sarcastically replied.

"Hey, don't worry. The crew here is straight and standing tall. Besides, there is a bunch of us here from the old training company." He rattled off the names of men I had trained.

I was something of an oddity to them. They all stopped by to talk if they were ambulatory or to pass on the conversation to those who weren't. All seemed surprised that I, an officer, had suffered the same fate as they.

At first I puzzled over this. But I began to believe the reason they found it surprising was that I was the first example of an authority figure they had known who was also capable of being destroyed.

Whatever our rank, we were now equal in physical pain and took comfort in each other's company.

All of us in the ward helped each other. One formed friendships with the men in the beds around him. The men who could walk would help other men out of bed to go to the latrine or to go to therapy. The men with hands would feed those who had no hands or no use of their hands. The men in wheelchairs would carry trays from bed to bed and act as a courier service. The men with eyes would describe the ward to the men who were blind. The men without voices joined in communicating with the other men by using facial expressions and hand movements. The men with no faces or partial faces were reassured by men with faces that they didn't look as bad as they thought and were quickly assimilated into the group. The men with no legs displayed their agility by swinging with their arms up on the frames above each bed that were used to support the pulleys for traction on broken or amputated limbs. There they would perch joking and keeping up the spirits of those men who could not move. All of us had something in common—we were wounded and fresh from combat.

But certain men were unapproachable. Regardless of the nature of their wounds, self-pity had eaten away at them, destroying their spirit. They rebuffed all overtures of friendship and turned in on themselves, wallowing in the acid of their bitterness.

In making an attempt to bring these soldiers into our lives, we would put up with a certain amount of rebuff because we knew the despair they felt. However, we theorized that if men who were worse off could make it, then these men who wouldn't had chosen a bad course. We slowly had to abandon them to themselves for fear they would drag us into their bitterness.

Each man's road back was torturous enough. Only when we were stronger would we dare reenter the maze in an attempt to salvage a lost brother. Many of us today, in the 1980s, are still trying to draw our comrades out of that maze of mental disorientation and physical pain brought about by war. But back in 1968 we were too uncertain of our own lives and too close to death to risk what we had recovered.

How We Survived

We concentrated on ourselves and then those next to us. The man on my left was a nineteen-year-old corporal. He told me what had happened to him.

His squad of ten men had been cut off when their company had had to retreat under heavy attack. He had been shot through the hand, losing two fingers and a thumb. He had been shot in the neck, the back, and the shoulder. The North Vietnamese Army overran his squad and he played dead to keep from being executed. He had so much blood on his body from his wounds that he looked dead.

While listening to his tale, I could see that the fear of the moment was still strong within him. It had happened only a few days before.

"I tell you, sir, I thought I had had it. The dinks overran us and I just lay there like I was dead. All of the guys had been hit and were crying or moaning from their wounds. The dinks just walked among us emptying their rifles into whoever was still alive. I was so scared. I knew they were going to kill me. They were stripping the bodies of rings and watches and wallets. When they got to me I lay as still as I could. One of them reached down and grabbed my shoulder to roll me over on my back. He slid my watch over my blasted hand and wiped the blood from it on my fatigue jacket. He picked up my other hand and yanked my ring off my finger. God! I thought I was dead. I just knew he would tell I was breathing! He threw my hand back across my body and kicked me real hard in the neck.

"Another guy was lying across the lower part of my body and he was moaning. He had some bad wounds and was practically unconscious. The dink turned him over and fired a burst into him. The bullets just missed my legs. I had blood all over me from my own wounds and the other guy's so I looked dead enough that they didn't waste any bullets on finishing me off. They took off chasing after the rest of the company.

"After a while I got up and followed after them to see if I could hook up with my company again. Shit! There was everything on the ground from the retreating company, C-rations, ammo, bloody bandages, and all sorts of equipment lying all over the gound. It was easy to follow them. I staggered from tree to tree and wandered in a daze half the time. Suddenly I saw some soldiers ahead of me dash behind cover. I thought they were the enemy so I jumped into the bushes. But they yelled at me because they had recognized me. I ran forward and fell right into their arms. They were from my platoon. I don't know how I managed to get through the dinks but I did and I want to tell you that I was happy. Those goddamn dinks! Executing us like that. Jesus I was scared!'' He lay back on his pillow, tired from the exertion of telling this story and the memory of his fears.

The man on my right had lost his legs above the knees because the man in front of him on patrol had stepped on a booby-trapped 105 shell. That soldier in front had simply disappeared in the blast but the shrapnel had torn the legs off this man. He never talked much, mostly stared at the wall opposite his bed.

There were other men close around me who became part of our fluid group.

I had never seen a combat hospital ward except in the movies, and on film the wounds were always freshly bandaged and healed quickly. But now, I knew better. Nothing shocked me now. I had seen a Vietnamese look incredulously at his intestines lying on the ground next to him. I had seen an American soldier's skull split by an AK-47 bullet, spilling his brains out over his fatigue jacket. I had seen an American soldier blown in half. I had seen an American soldier totally blended into the wreckage of his truck as it ran over a land mine. Blown-off legs and arms had become so common as to seem routine. Blood pouring from numerous holes in the bodies of friends became a fact of life.

When a body's integrity was violated the body tended to erupt into a hideous caricature of itself instead of just folding in and quietly falling. The Vietnam war was no movie.

In the hospital wards I became even more intimately aware of this. I was amazed at the almost innumerable ways and places in which the human body could be wounded. Most astounding to me was the punishment a human being could take and survive.

Being our own society in the hospital, we were not self-conscious about our wounds. They were our entry fee, our bona fides. And we were recovering. Our minds maintained clarity for longer periods of time. We helped each other. The hospital staff helped us. Our society was all of a piece. But essentially we were hiding and we knew it. We would not be able to hide forever.

The USO had groups touring the hospitals to cheer us up. These groups were our first link to the outside. I remember two of the groups particularly well. One was a barbershop quartet. A hurried message by the staff informed us that entertainment would shortly arrive in the ward. We were excited. What could it be? Change of any kind was a welcome diversion. We heard the singing as the group of four men entered the ward at the far end and slowly progressed down the other aisle. They would stop every tenth bed or so to do a song. As they started up our aisle, I studied their faces to see how they took what they were seeing.

They measured up very well. Their harmonizing songs were a touch of home, a lot like the records my mom used to play. The quartet moved up past my bed to stand across from my local friends and myself. We smiled in silence through their repertoire. Their courage must have been great to enter our ward with smiling faces, singing songs of home. For those of us without hands or the ability to clap, our bright faces were the only applause the group received; it seemed to be quite enough.

The other group I remember because they had once been my heroes.

Four professional football players toured our ward to stop and talk to the different soldiers. One of those men was Bart Starr. I resolved not to ask him to stop by my bed because there were men much worse off than I whom Bart Starr could talk to, and I did not want to take him away from those men. However, I did hope he would stop voluntarily. I had gone through high school and college watching him quarterback for Green Bay on television every Sunday. During those days I knew that someone like Bart Starr was as far removed from me as the moon.

I thought it was ironic that I had to have less than a perfect body in order to meet a man whom I admired and who made his living with his body.

Suddenly he was standing next to my bed. I do not remember our conversation exactly. But I remember Bart Starr's face and his eyes. The ward had shaken him. His face was straining in its effort to maintain composure, but the eyes could not be controlled. They mirrored the shock, the pity, the horror, and the hopeless despair of one who has seen the ravaged bodies of young men forever crippled, and has realized the vulnerability of his own.

I lay there with one arm gone, the other one useless. He could be thinking, "There but for the grace of God go I," but maybe not—nothing so trivial.

What Starr did next proved to me that he was not a false person. He conquered everything in his face, smiled at me, and reached forward to touch my shoulder.

"Did you play any sports in high school?"

"Yes sir, I did. In football I was an outside linebacker and lettered two years. I ran the mile and half-mile in track and lettered three years."

"Did you like it?"

"I sure did. I love sports."

"Did you have someone in your grade or school who wasn't able to participate in sports because they had a disease or an accident?"

"Yes, there were some. A few of my classmates had polio, and I have a cousin who went to another school who was born with a club foot."

"What is your cousin like?"

"He doesn't let anything get him down. He does everything. His brothers fight with him and he fights right back!''

"I see here your name is Fred. Well Fred, you've gotten to do a lot in life your classmates and cousin have never had the chance to do. They didn't let their disabilities get them down. Now you have to show them and yourself the same kind of courage they have had all these years. If you never give up, you will do it! What do you think?''

"I can do it. I've already started. I just have to get used to it and I'm pretty adaptable anyway.''

"Okay, I know you can. I'll go check on some of these other men. I'll see you sometime.''

He went on down the line of men while I lay there wondering if I really had that kind of courage.

Would I be able truly to overcome my handicap? I felt very uncertain about the future. But I would do what I had to do. At that moment I loved Bart Starr.

There were television sets in the ward that could be moved up next to a bed where two or maybe three soldiers could see the picture. Because of some crazy agreement (crazy to us, anyway) between the Japanese and American governments, no U.S. Armed Forces television shows could be aired in Japan, at least in the hospital. So we watched Japanese stations in, of course, the Japanese language.

But since a lot of American television adventure and sit-coms had been sold to the Japanese we were able to watch Matt Dillon, Chester, Kitty, and Doc speaking Japanese to each other. There were also a lot of Huckleberry Hound cartoons and, although I had always hated them, they seemed to gain something in Japanese.

The Japanese produced a lot of their own shows based on the Samurai warriors. We identified with the warriors and each show had an avid audience of wounded soldiers who gathered around the television set to watch the often-tragic shows.

One thing was the same—endless ads—seemingly even

more than we had been used to back home.

One day there was an excited hubbub at the far end of the ward as an officer and two MPs entered and were met by the ward master. After a consultation, the ward master turned to a nurse standing next to him and asked a question.

All of us in the ward were staring at the group, wondering what the devil was going on. The nurse pointed in our direction, whereupon the officer and the two MPs hurried down the aisle toward us followed by the ward master and his crew.

"Jesus," the man on my left quizzed, "are they coming to take us back to Nam?"

The group stopped two beds up from us in our row. The officer asked the wounded man in that bed if he had smuggled a weapon into the ward and did he have it now?

We were surprised at such a dumb question, but amazed when the man nodded yes.

The MPs pulled back the mattress to uncover an AK-47 combat assault rifle with magazine pouches. One of them pulled it out from under the mattress and professionally checked the chamber and barrel to make sure the weapon was clear.

It was the first enemy rifle we had seen since leaving combat—a very superior weapon, better than an M-16.

But what in hell was a wounded soldier doing with an AK-47? The MPs and their officer had recorded the man's name, service number, and other required information, but beyond that they were uncertain what to do. The man couldn't be arrested. He had been punished quite enough by his wounds if punishment was called for. Besides, the only reason the man had it was as a war souvenir and he wanted to make sure it made it back to "The World" in his possession. And, another thing, he could not have possibly hidden the AK-47 all the way from Nam without some collusion from everyone starting from the dust-off crew right through to the orderlies who had brought him into the ward and transferred him from the litter to the bed.

Furthermore, he was going to make a fuss. He demanded that the rifle be listed as his personal possession (he claimed to have killed the enemy soldier who owned it) and that it be transported to wherever he went back in the world.

The officer wasn't sure about that. In fact, he wasn't sure some law hadn't been violated, but he wasn't going to discuss it in the ward. He took the rifle and ammo with him and turned and marched out, followed by the MPs. It turned out that one of the other nurses had tipped off the ward master when she discovered the rifle laying next to him.

I couldn't blame her. Having an assault rifle with ammo in a ward of so much pain and misery could have turned into a disaster. Many of us were on the far edge of sanity. Acting as a catalyst, the drugs and our nightmares could have caused us to destroy the enemy all around us if we had the opportunity of getting our hands on a weapon. And who was the enemy?

In early February, a week or so after I had arrived at the 249th, a very familiar face showed up. He rolled a wheelchair through a door connecting our ward to another ward and hollered across to me, "Delta 1-6, how the fuck are you?"

"Bob, what the fuck, over!" mimicking a common saying among soldiers, I laughed in relief at seeing my RTO (radio-telephone operator). He had been right behind me when I had stepped on the land mine. It had maimed him from the waist down in the front. I remembered as I lay on the trail that blood had covered him like a sheet. When we had been loaded onto the dust-off, I had not been able to see him because he was in the tier above me. However, when we were lying on the cots in the MASH unit he was being worked on in the next cot and that had been the last I had seen of him. Now he rolled up next to me.

"Shit, sir! I thought you had had it! You were really fucked up! Goddamn it, sir! That fucking Bouncing Betty exploded out of the ground behind you and it was moving so fast it was just a gray blur and before I could move or even yell that fucking dink motherfucker exploded! It knocked me back on my ass! I thought I was zapped for sure. Nothing had ever hurt that bad ever!"

"You mean you actually saw the mine explode out of the ground? Jesus! Remember that lieutenant over in Alpha Company who stepped on a Bouncing Betty and it exploded out of the ground in front of him but the main charge didn't go off so the mine just flew right on up past his head a foot or so and then fell back right at his feet? Remember he was so fucking in shock that they had to call in a chopper to fly him back for a rest? Well, I have to wonder why that didn't happen to us. We must not be living right."

"Probably because we were so fucking hard-core, sir. Those dinks had to send in their best land-mine team to finally get us. Shit! We were the best platoon in the battalion."

"Fucking A."

"It was a lick on us, sir!"

"Yeah, a fucking lick! . . . Hey they saved your legs!"

"Just barely! That fucking Doc back in 'Nam was going to cut them off for Christ's sake; but I told him I would kill him if he did!"

"His name wasn't Colonel Ellis was it?"

"Naw, I don't know what the fuck his name was. I wonder how the platoon is doing without you and me there, sir."

"I don't know, but Marly's platoon sergeant now or he was when he left, and he's squared away so the guys should be okay. They did run into trouble. Gary got his legs blown off and Vince got blown in half and four other guys got hit. I saw Gary in Qui Nhon and he looked okay except for his legs, which were blown off above the knees. It was a lick."

"That whole 'Nam is number fucking 10, Delta 1–6, and that's no shit!" Bob was good company.

One particular thing that happened while Bob was there put him in excellent spirits. Bob generally hated all officers except me and he took tremendous glee in anything that confirmed his belief that officers were "ignorant assholes." Bob's platoon nickname was "The Savage" because of his ruthlessness in dealing with both the dinks and anyone else whom he didn't like.

One night before lights out he pushed his wheelchair up to my bed, his face lit with an unholy glee.

"Sir, sir, you gotta see this! They just brought a new patient into my ward this evening and they put him right next to me. And guess what, sir? He's a fucking colonel. But the best thing is that he zapped himself. That stupid motherfucker came down out of the sky in his special officer's chopper and walked right into his officer's chopper's tail rotor! Yeeeee! Fucked him up! He's lost an eye and part of his head and he may not make it!"

"Goddamn, Bob! What's the matter with you? That poor son of a bitch is hurting just like us and just because he's a colonel doesn't make him a dink for Christ's sake!"

"I know, sir, I know, but shiiiit! A colonel? I didn't know they ever got zapped. Now I know they don't get it by the dinks but they give it to themselves. You think he'll get a purple heart? I bet he gets a purple heart. The shamming motherfucker. All colonels are shamming."

A silence developed as we thought over our close brushes with authorities who had threatened our close-knit combat unit. One instance in particular made me smile. "Remember that dink police chief's Honda-50 you threw in the creek? You about got me shot!"

"Shit yeah." Bob threw his head back and we laughed together at the memory.

The memory of my earlier effort to walk had faded and I was determined to walk now regardless of how painful it was. Each day I would have an orderly pull me upright and help me out of bed. Although with his help I could only shuffle a few yards before the intense pain forced me back into bed, I was happy at the progress.

It seemed a good idea to go with Bob to visit the colonel by walking the fifty feet from my bed through a connecting door into the other ward that spread out like a spike from the nurse's station, which was the hub. Much to my chagrin, however, I could not manage more than a few steps, so I was rolled over in a wheelchair by an orderly to meet him but the colonel was in such sorry shape that he didn't respond very well to our questions. His name was on the card at the end of his bed. I don't think he knew his own name at that point. But Bob was satisfied that I had seen with my own eyes a colonel who had walked into his tail rotor.

After lights out there was never any quiet. The period set aside for sleep was eerily alive with the sounds of troubled men murmuring and babbling in the night. The dim light from the nurse's station at the end of the ward allowed enough visibility for them to move among us at night administering shots or calming us down. But the feeble light did something else which I'm sure had never been planned. It kept us from complete darkness. Ever since I had been hit there had been some light spreading out over the wards from the nurse's station.

It was a Godsend.

I would awake in the night, startled and confused as to where I was and why I was in such agony, my body sheathed in a cocoon of tormenting pain. As I fought to unscramble my muddled mind my eyes would trace the soft light emanating from the darkness. The light came from a glass-enclosed cubicle at the end of the ward. A glass door stood open to admit sounds.

Sitting there, bathed in a pool of light cast from a desk lamp, would be the night nurse, dressed in white, reading or filling out reports or writing a letter. This peaceful vision had a restorative effect by calming me in those first moments of fresh, unorganized terror, of finding only a stump of bandaged flesh where my left arm should have been. Each time I woke, the loss staggered me. But the glow of light held me fast.

To have faced pitch blackness would have been devastating. Even with the light it was bad enough. The sounds of men in the night were worse in the ward at the 249th. We were being pulled off the heavy drugs to avoid addiction; therefore, our minds were more aware. But I could get only an hour's sleep after my shot before the pain awakened me. I would lie staring at the shadows on the ceiling cast by the nurse's light and wonder for the millionth time if the pain would ever stop.

Around me men moaned. To occupy the night I tried to determine which sounds came from which man. In the hundred-man ward there were many different sounds.

Men would still occasionally die, though not at the pace they had at Chu Lai and Qui Nhon. They mostly died at night, just like before, and we could tell when it was going to happen. It was a sixth sense, when a man was giving up; we just knew.

The death of a fellow soldier in combat or later in the hospitals was a sledgehammer blow to me and the other men. We didn't discuss it much except in warrior's terms: He got zapped with an AK-47; American artillery fired short and two guys bought it; that ambush was a fucking lick; the burn case died last night; or the guy from the 101st Airborne with the crushed chest didn't make it.

In spite of the cavalier way in which we discussed death,

each man had to face in solitude the question of how the nearness of death would affect him. Would he be haunted by nightmares, become guilt-ridden, self-pitying, weak, cowardly, ineffective, timid? Or would he become strong, aggressive, fearless, confident, mature, philosophical? Regardless of all, would he be defeated?

All of us would spend the rest of our lives discovering the answers.

On 31 January 1968, reports of major attacks launched by the Vietcong throughout South Vietnam spread an electric shock wave through the ward. This was good news. We agreed that when those fucking dinks came out of their holes and fought us in the open we would kick their asses. They had made their mistake! Superior American firepower would destroy the enemy.

We talked about the attacks and lamented on our misfortune not to be back there participating in the battles. Someone said that it was just like the gooks to launch an attack during a truce.

"What truce was that?" another man asked.

A soldier answered, "It's their New Year's celebration; Tet, I think they call it."

I continued to have daily surgery. After surgery I would come to in the post-op room leading my platoon in combat. Once I became aware of where I was I would be disappointed, wanting desperately to return to my dream. The only nice thing about the surgery was having my pain shots increased afterward. I depended on the strong pain shots for two reasons: They numbed the pain and they allowed my world unlimited freedom. I was acquiring a hunger for drugs.

Little did I know how dependent on drugs I had become. I might not have cared, but something was nagging my conscience. My greatest asset was the will to live. Drugs destroy the will so the fact that I didn't care should have been a warning; but as with all cases of the mind during this traumatic period in a wounded soldier's life, no one explained these things to us. Either we figured it out ourselves or we were lost.

I did get my first real bath at the 249th. I was put into a wheelchair and pushed to a therapy room that had a whirlpool. The pain of being lifted by three orderlies and put into the whirlpool did not diminish the ecstasy of feeling clean for the first time in two months. The scabs, dead skin, puss, and corruption swirled away from my body making me feel like a new man. I loved that whirlpool.

Transfer Notification

On 8 February 1968, I received notice of transfer to "The World"—a place in Denver, Colorado, called Fitzsimmons Army Hospital. I had been asked shortly before where I wanted to go and had asked for the Great Lakes area because my family was from Indiana. When I was told I was going to Denver, I began to feel I was in the regular army again. Even a wounded soldier's request for a duty station was filled out on a dream sheet! Some things never change. But I was changing.

The men I mentioned earlier from Fort Gordon, Georgia, were all ambulatory wounded and they decided to take me to a movie on base as a going-away treat. Padding a wheelchair with three pillows, they dressed me in the blue hospital robes, and about five of them rolled me through the dusk toward the theater to see *Point Blank* starring Lee Marvin. We were happy to be doing something familiar and safe. They rolled me right down to the front row where I sat in the wheelchair in the aisle.

We were all so gun shy that every time Lee Marvin shot

someone with his 357 Magnum we flinched. To us, sitting in
the front row was like being in the movie itself.

It was the first violent movie I had seen since I had left
for the war. But the violence didn't bother me, only the
noise. All of us flinched throughout the movie—a survival
reflex from 'Nam which decreed that any different noise demanded unthinking, instant reaction by the body. All soldiers
from any war are familiar with the survival reflex.

The movie made me think about the reasons we die. The
meaning of death was in its importance to the survivors. If
we were right in our reasons for being in a war, our deaths
were honorable. But if stories of the anti-war movement we
had heard about back in the world were true, then our deaths
were becoming dishonorable. And to those combat men still
alive, if death lost its importance then the reason for death
became meaningless and therefore a waste.

Point Blank was not a memorable movie but I remember
it well as the first taste of home. Afterward, the guys rolled
me back to the ward. I did not talk much because of my pain.
I was feeling nauseous again, and I was silent, deep in my
thoughts about death.

The night before I was to be transferred back to the world
the nurses invited me and some of the other officers to a
hail-and-farewell party being given for a doctor. This was
exciting news: escape from the bed! All of the men I had
trained and the orderlies who had become friends worked at
getting me ready for my big date. I was determined to go
out no matter how sick I was or how much pain the exertion
would cause me. I wanted out!

I could walk for short distances now so I thought I could
handle going out. Even those who couldn't go took great
delight in helping me get prepared. Someone donated a pair
of pants, an orderly supplied a sweater, one man had a shirt,
and the duty nurses got me a new pair of slippers. All of the

guys that could move pretty well helped me wash, shave, and get dressed, and took as much pride in my appearance as if they were the ones going out. Even though I was an invalid, they all agreed I should be able to dance if I drank enough. I would not be able to grasp a bottle or glass with my bandaged hand but I could suck liquor through a straw.

The only sour note came innocently from an orderly who was particularly friendly and helpful to all of us. He was the one who had supplied the sweater. He was standing to the side of the bed, choreographing the efforts of the other men dressing me. The bandages were bulky, making it difficult to pull on sleeves and trousers. Also, stiffened arm and legs were forced to bend and stretch to degrees my body no longer recognized as normal.

When the men finished the details of zipping and buttoning, the orderly stepped in to smooth out the creases, set up the "gig" line, and add any finishing touches.

For the first time since August I stood dressed in civilian clothes, acutely aware of the empty sleeve hanging loosely at my left side.

I felt uncomfortable and embarrassed to be without an arm. The sudden insight that I would be like this the rest of my life plunged me into a deep melancholy.

The orderly bustled around pinning the empty shirt and sweater sleeve into a neat fold at the end of the stump. He patted the fold and cheerfully remarked, "As soon as you get back to the States, Lieutenant, they'll have one of those artificial arms on you in nothing flat!"

He could not know how I dreaded that—an ugly, awkward, plastic arm and metal hook being forever part of my body. I shivered at the prospect of people staring at it. But I looked up into the circle of expectant faces, smiling from the fun we all had getting me dressed, and instinctively knew I would destroy all our fantasies for the evening if I even hinted at my fears.

I smiled back at him. "You're right. When I get that arm there won't be any stopping me. I'll do everything I ever did before. Would you believe I can't wait to pinch some girl's ass with a hook?"

That's the spirit we all wanted to hear. I even believed it myself a bit. The comment got us to talking about women and cars and what wild adventures we would have when we got back in the world.

We sounded very brave.

As 8:00 P.M.(2000 hours) rolled around the whole ward anticipated the great time I was going to have and the raunchy stories ran rampant. I sat in a chair conserving my energy, smiling, and kidding with the guys as I wondered if I could make it through a party. I also wondered at the strangeness of human beings that could kill one day, be wounded the next, and still look forward to a night of entertainment.

Finally the nurses arrived and amid much good-natured ribbing of the ward we were loaded into a Ford Mustang. The officers' club was only a few blocks away. After the short drive we were guided into the club and sat at a long table in the dining and dance room. One of my nurse friends on duty that night had given me her "special" shot which she said was guaranteed to keep me going all night. I felt like I could go all week.

I don't remember a party I enjoyed quite as much as that one. The entertainment was a Japanese group that sang country and western songs in English. This was the only English they knew. They were dressed in bright red, green, gold, and blue sequined uniforms with Indianapolis-style racing cars sewn onto the fronts of their outfits. I don't believe they took one break all night. They sang all the country songs I loved, but the two I remember best were "Wabash Cannon Ball" and "Back Home Again in Indiana."

The men and women at the party were doctors, nurses, administrative officers, and wounded officers. Wounded officers made up the majority of the crowd, or at least they were the most visible to me.

Down the length of my table I observed wounded men dressed in uniforms, "civies," and hospital robes drinking and enjoying life. We had almost lost it and we were intense in our efforts to squeeze out what we could tonight.

A few times during the evening I found myself feeling mildly sexual about the women at the party. I was too full of drugs and hurt to be much excited by those thoughts, but knowing they still prowled around was heartening.

If a man could move he could dance. I danced slow dances (couldn't handle the fast ones) until the pain stopped me; I then sat at a table and drank with my newfound friends. The party lasted until the early morning hours and we would not have quit then except for bed check and duty hours.

When I returned to the ward some of the men woke up and wanted to know what it was like. Fantastic, I said. The retelling was almost as much fun as the party itself. I was exhausted and feeling pain to a nauseous degree, but the party was worth it.

Much too early in the morning I was awakened and transferred to a litter where I lay in the hall while a consignment of wounded was put together. I bid my friends goodbye and watched in silence as people hurried back and forth trying to sort everyone out.

We were loaded onto the familiar olive-drab bus in tiers. I had a window and was able to see as we moved to the airport through the impossibly narrow streets of the Japanese city located next to the 249th. Masses of people thronged, staring at us. I stared back in return. I had been watching their television shows so long I felt I knew them a lot better than they knew me.

The bus inched along through heavy traffic, the driver starting and stopping with a jolt which set my teeth on edge.

Like a stream of buffalo the Japanese flowed around us. They would look up at the Americans staring back at them. I was curious about what they must have been thinking while watching a busload of wounded foreign soldiers passing by on a street in their town.

I wished I had been well enough to visit outside the hospital and to have known them better. "But," I sighed, "they're only dinks. I want to go home."

At the runway, I was loaded onto a large four-engine jet, a C-141 "starlifter," and given a shot, and I do not remember one moment of the flight back to the world.

The next day, the Medivac stopped at Travis Air Force Base in California where we were unloaded to be distributed to hospitals across the United States. I spent the night at a hospital in a pain-filled drugged daze. Half out of my head, I rambled on about my platoon as I guided and directed them through one fire fight after another. There was one other wounded man in my room. His wife was standing by his bed.

I thought that was strange until it dawned on me that I was back in the world. Here everything was possible.

As I was loaded onto the Medivac flight the next morning for the final leg to Denver, I resolved to be conscious when we arrived so I wouldn't miss the band and welcoming committee. I had expected it at each stop and there had been none. But I had rationalized each disappointment. Since Denver would be my final stop I knew they would be waiting for us—just like movies and books had always portrayed.

CHAPTER 5

Fitzsimmons
Army Hospital

Denver, Colorado
11 February–30 April 1968

As the pilot eased the Medivac onto the runway at Buckley
Airfield outside of Denver, Colorado, reversing the engines
to slow the aircraft as we rolled toward a taxiway, all of us
talked excitedly about finally being home. Those who had
windows were describing Colorado to the rest of us. Craning
my head around on my litter I could see nothing but what I
had seen for the two-hour flight, row upon row of wounded
on both sides of the aircraft, some thirty of us. Forty or fifty
of the less seriously wounded were sitting in two rows of
seats up the middle of the floor.

Finally the aircraft braked to a stop. What sort of reception would be waiting for us? The gigantic doors of the aircraft opened to admit bright shafts of sunlight. U. S. Air
Force and Army personnel streamed on board to flow among
us checking names, writing on forms, aiding the ambulatory
out of the aircraft, supervising as each litter was unlocked
from its brackets to be carried out. These were the sounds
we were accustomed to.

I was carried down the ramp and my litter placed on the
runway in a line with other litters. The bright sunlight blinded
me at first but gradually I was able to look at the bluest sky
I had ever seen.

A colonel and a Red Cross lady leaned over me where I lay on the runway waiting to be loaded onto a bus for transporting to Fitzsimmons Army Hospital.

They were asking me questions, welcoming me to the United States and Colorado. Their smiles told me I was in the world for sure. For the first time in almost six months I did not have to worry about being shot, ambushed, stepping on a land mine, tripping a booby trap, or being wary of civilians. I was back in the United States, safe at last.

This had to be it! The official welcoming home. Still sedated from the flight I raised my head.

"Is there a band?" I asked.

"What? What did you say, Lieutenant?" The Red Cross lady leaned closer.

"A band, where is it?"

"There isn't any band, Lieutenant. We never have a band."

Uncertain now and slightly embarrassed, I hesitated, "Well, you know, a . . . a . . . welcoming committee. Sort of to show us that people are glad to have us back . . ." My voice dwindled off. Why didn't she know what I meant? A welcome back band was so obvious. Especially for wounded soldiers. But I did not want to appear ungrateful.

The colonel, a major, and the Red Cross lady looked down at me in the bright Colorado sun. The major cleared his throat.

"We are the welcoming committee, Lieutenant, and I can assure you that we are very happy to welcome you back to the United States. And since we are military people we know better than anyone what you men have gone through so I guess it's only proper that we be the ones to welcome you back."

I smiled back. He was right. Whatever happened, my military family was always there and always would be. If no one else cared, they would.

"Hey, you're right; who needs a band anyway," I murmured.

We were soon loaded onto the buses for the short trip to Fitzsimmons. After arriving, the bus backed up to the rear doors of the large eight-story hospital where familiar teams of the hospital staff waited for us.

Fitzsimmons is a mammoth, seventeen-hundred-bed hospital that was built in 1921 in Aurora, a suburb of Denver, and named for the first American medical officer killed after America entered World War I. The hospital sits in the middle of one hundred sixty acres, surrounded by a number of two-story buildings on three sides. These buildings provided out-patient wards for the overflow of wounded, barracks for the duty staff, the P.X., movie theater, commissary, officers' club and non-commissioned officers' (NCO) club, laundry, barbershop, library, and extra offices for administrative and finance personnel. Besides the buildings, the grounds contained a stockade for prisoners, a red-and-white checked water tower, a power plant, a landing pad for the Medivac helicopter, a parade ground, an eighteen-hole golf course, and a picnic area. A high fence enclosed the whole area, broken only by two main gates, one on Colfax Avenue and one on Peoria Street.

As with any army base, Fitzsimmons could have been dropped anywhere in the world and would have remained a cohesive, functioning unit. Any American army base is a microcosm, self-contained, capable of surviving on its own. There is enough water, food, medical supplies, and other essentials to last for days or weeks. A contingency plan exists for everything from a riot to a nuclear attack.

An enclosed society was fine with me. I felt safe within the boundaries of the army's little world. Security was still my great need.

I was assigned to Ward 5 West, one of the wards that specialized in amputees. The end of that wing was a large open bay with four rows of beds spread across its length, and a large number of windows arrayed on three sides. I was still unused to windows. In five and a half months of combat I had not seen one glass window in any of the dirt, bamboo, and grass hootches (dwellings for humans, no matter how primitive) that the Vietnamese lived in.

I had gone through the usual rigamarole of having my blood tested and lost my usual argument with the nurse and orderly about what the blood test would show. As I lay there staring at the ceiling a nurse named Pam bustled over. "Hey Lieutenant, why didn't you say something about the fact that you were an officer when you were put in this open ward?"

"What do you mean? Ever since I got hit no one ever said that my being an officer made any difference in where I was put. This is fine right next to the window. I can see clear out across the hospital grounds from here."

"Well, the open ward is for enlisted men. Since you're an officer you get a private room." She started to roll my bed away from the window.

"Wait a minute. I'm fine right here. It doesn't make any difference to me. Besides, there are guys around me to talk to in here."

"It may not make any difference to you, Lieutenant, but it does to the army. They say you get a private room so it's a private room you get."

She rolled me past the nurse's station into a private room on the north side of the hall. The room had a bathroom, a closet, a television set—and a window.

It was time for my shot. Afterward I floated above my bed listening to the commercial jets taking off from Stapleton, Denver's airport. Each jet reminded me that I was safe. People were on those jets bound for pleasure or business. They didn't have to worry about being shot down.

I was obsessed with the difference between Vietnam and

America. Like all Americans, I had grown up taking for granted a simple idea—that peace was the natural state in my own community.

In Vietnam, there was no peace. Everyone lived in fear— the North Vietnamese Army, Vietcong, ARVNs, Rough Puffs (local militia), Americans, and every stranger. Buildings could be booby-trapped, vehicles could be packed with explosives, and even the land itself could be filled with mines. Nothing was safe. Death might at any moment reach out and casually smash all in its path. Control over life disappeared. Death was the master and anyone who failed to study death, in order to avoid it, did not survive.

I had broken a rule: I had used a gateway twice. By day it was safe to stroll through the gate; that night it had changed to a gateway of death.

As evening time of my first day at Fitzsimmons drifted through the weakening powers of my last drug shot, I became aware of a good-looking nurse standing in my doorway.

"Heyyy, who are you?"

"I'm Lieutenant Jan Gish and I'm putting your name in the slot out here, Lieutenant. Here, you want to see the card before I put it up?" She came into the room and held the card so I could read it.

Second Lieutenant Frederick Downs, Jr., 11 February 1968.

"February 11th! That's today? I was hit exactly one month ago." Lieutenant Gish inserted the card into the slot alongside my door and told me she would be back to feed me at supper time.

"You can feed me as long as you don't serve me any more liquid diets. I'm sick of green jello and whatever that crappy soup is!" I hated the very sight of green jello. Someone in Washington, D.C., had decreed that a liquid diet must include green jello for lunch and supper and, because of the injuries to my lower intestinal tract, I had been started on a liquid diet a couple of weeks ago. I yearned for a real meal.

And I got one, that night. As Lieutenant Gish patiently spooned food into my mouth, I thought for the thousandth time what a miserable existence I was living that I could not even feed myself. The doctors had assured me they would not have to amputate my right arm. However, they were unsure of the extent of the nerve damage. The arm and hand were useless now, bound up as they were in thick bandages. I was disgusted.

"Fucking dinks!"

Lieutenant Gish stopped the spoon midway between the plate and my mouth. "What did you say Lieutenant Downs?"

"Uhhh, er, well, it was just a 'Nam term for the enemy. Sorry about that."

"Oh." The spoon approached toward my mouth.

I thought to myself, "Shit, not only can't I help myself, I can't even swear about it." This situation was Number Fucking 10. I smiled at that. At the same time, I was staring at Lieutenant Gish's breasts. They looked great.

The next spoonful of food was stuck into my chin.

"Sorry about that," she said.

"That's all right, I didn't have my mind on it."

"I'll be glad to report that you're starting to heal, Lieutenant Downs."

After she had finished feeding me she left to help another wounded man. I lay there listening to the sounds outside my door. For the first time since stepping on the land mine I was in a room alone. I could see people walking by my open door, but no one stopped to talk. I was lonely. Regardless of the suffering I had seen, regardless of my drugged state, always before I felt the power of people near me, and heard them talk to the other men close by my cot, and they could talk to me if they needed to. Amid all of the pain and terror, we had had each other to cling to, and the nurse's station had always been within sight. Out in the hallway was life; here in my room were only my thoughts. What did it matter if I was an officer. It was not good to be by myself. Later, perhaps, when I was healthier, I could use the loneliness, but not now. Now I needed companionship.

The noise of television, radios, and people, and the lights that flooded the hospital, all combined to push me steadily down into a deep depression. All of that life was there and I was no part of it.

After lights out I lay quietly, trying to focus all of my being into the drug I had just been given. My skin was now so porous from needles that some of this night's drug had run back out of the hole when the needle had been withdrawn. I had asked for another shot to make up for the lost drug, but the night nurse refused, saying that it was dangerous to give me more without knowing how much had not entered my system.

I had not had a restful night since being wounded. The phantom pain in my stump had become very bothersome, almost more than the pain from the rest of my body. I was worn out. I wanted one good night of rest. As the ward quieted my wish for sleep became a prayer. Neither worked.

I decided on a desperate measure—to trick the night nurse into giving me a pain shot. I looked over the side of my bed. Of course. I would fake falling out of bed. But when I tried, the stitches in my buttocks and legs pulled taut causing me to cry out. Losing my balance, I lurched over and landed on a trash can with my shoulder. The racket of the can being knocked across the room and my yell brought the night nurse running. She was an older lady who had probably seen every trick in the book from patients trying to get drugs.

I was convincing. But my trick had turned into a disaster

for me. I really was in unbearable pain as I lay writhing on the floor.

She called out for an orderly and told someone to have the duty officer summon a doctor. She and the orderly lifted me back onto the bed. She then snapped up the bed railing to keep me from falling out again. When the doctor arrived he gave me a shot that still couldn't completely cover the pain I had caused myself.

Clenching my teeth I stared at the ceiling thinking that the month of pain killers had scrambled my brains for me to pull such a foolish stunt.

At 0100 hours the nurse gave me some strong sleeping tablets, but I couldn't drift off for three hours.

At 0600 hours the staff woke us up for our medicine. I wanted to sleep on, but I was still in the army.

Growing Complexities: Psychological and Physical

Later that morning Pam, a good-humored, plump nurse from Indiana, rolled a wheelchair into the room to take me down for an X-ray examination and more tests. I was still slightly delirious after the night, to say nothing of the cumulative effects of a month of pain, surgery, drugs, psychic trauma, and little sleep. It was easier and easier to let myself slip over the edge out of control of my mind. I was worried about that because the only freedom I had left was freedom of the mind through drugs.

The nurse rolled me down the hall past other rooms where wounded lay, to the central core of the hospital where the elevators were located. She stopped in front of the doors and pushed a button for an elevator—so normal, so routine. Everything was coming too fast. No one had explained to me what I might expect, where I would be going, what the procedures were, what would happen to me.

The doors opened onto a crowd of women, children, old men, and hospital workers. Up to now my world had only been wounded men and those who worked with wounded men, but now I was moving past pregnant women and people with colds, hangnails, pulled muscles, and other noncombat injuries.

I felt out of place. What do they see? A figure in a blue military robe, gaunt, humped over. A one-armed soldier sadly sitting in a wheelchair, or a proud combat infantry soldier brought low by the enemy but not defeated?

What amazed me was the constant rocking back and forth of my mind. All of us know the mind operates on different levels but never before the wound had I experienced such a sharp differentiation. It was strange to go from insanity to sanity and back again. I had difficulty coping with this because it was alien to my nature and I had not been prepared beforehand. I had been trained to treat a sucking chest wound, to perform a tracheotomy, to set a splint, to stop bleeding, to treat for shock, but no one had told me what a wounded mind was like.

To compound this oversight, there had been no provision by this vast medical machine, so superior technologically, to deal professionally with the psychological problems of the wounded. There was some professional help for the men classified as disturbed or brain injured, but for the vast majority of us there was nothing.

On the other hand, if the military was superior in any field of war, it was in the area of care of patients with physical damage. It was the best in the world. Therefore, if the psychological damage was not being treated, then it was because the professionals in that field had not brought it to the military's attention, or the military would have attacked the problem with the same fanaticism they had used to develop their medical care programs.

For instance, the tests that day showed I had five parasites and diseases picked up in Vietnam. Medicine was immediately prescribed to rid my body of them. The military spared no expense in the healing process. But more important for me were the special clinics, where the most up-to-date techniques, albeit a little experimental at times, were used.

Monday was stump clinic; Tuesday was hand clinic. On those days I waited my turn to be ushered into a room full of doctors. The doctor who was working on me for that particular disability would have me stand or sit in front of the other doctors while he described the treatment of my wound.

The chief doctor, Colonel Brown, stood a bit away acting as monitor while other doctors asked questions or suggested different procedures. I felt that this open forum was to my benefit because the doctor working on me had to justify his work before other doctors. If he was on the wrong track or if there was a better way, one of the twenty or so of his peers would come up with it. Colonel Brown was tough on the doctors and did not hesitate to call their attention to something he thought they should be doing. He protected us and we felt secure knowing he was watchdogging our treatment.

My legs had been saved. I was grateful for that. But the concern now was to return as much function as possible to my arm. The land mine had damaged the nerves, muscles, blood vessels, and tendons to such an extent that no one was sure how much, if any, function I would recover. All agreed that a good course would be to cover my right arm with skin grafts from wrist to elbow to offer me protection while the underlying tissues healed. The skin would come from the front of my legs. Back I would go for more surgery.

Goddamn! More surgery! More pain! More drugs! An unending chain that wore me down. I had weighed one hundred seventy pounds before I was wounded. I weighed one hundred twenty pounds now. And after all this time and all the operations, my hand still did not work.

The doctors and patients joked, only partly in jest, that if a doctor could get your hand to work well enough to hold a bottle of beer and wipe your ass, then you were successfully rehabilitated.

Life as an invalid was complex. The simplest functions—eating, defecating, urinating, drinking, switching on the television set, pulling the blanket up around my shoulders when I got chilly or prepared to go to sleep, and opening my mail—took a great deal of effort that involved the planning and cooperation of other people.

I was reminded again and again of the helplessness of not being able to use my hands. I was also a little worried after having seen the stark reality of my damaged hand and arm that the doctors had unveiled and explained to me (which the Filipino doctors at Clark had not), after I had arrived at Fitzsimmons. After the bandages were removed he and I examined the thin claw of my hand. One finger had a small piece of skin holding a knuckle to the rest of the finger, a large hole exposed the bones at the base of the thumb, and numerous small wounds were scattered over the hand, but most ominous of all was a long wound down the palm held together with wire stitching. Green fuzz was growing out of that wound.

"What's that green fuzz, Doc? That looks weird. I saw something like that growing out of baloney Mom left out once and she threw it away."

"Hmmmmm" was the only answer I got.

Shortly after, the operation was laid on.

As I rolled into the surgery room for the umpteenth time, I marveled at how little I knew about what was happening medically that would affect me for the rest of my life.

The surgery room was full of masked people in green gowns ready to do battle with the damage of my body. They stood in their assigned places while waiting for me to be rolled to a stop. Each person there had a specific job and, with little wasted movement, they started in on their tasks. I had already been given a prep shot back in my room an hour earlier, which I had been told by our orderly was supposed to settle me down.

Now I lay naked beneath the sheet ready for the next step. Intravenous tubes were hooked up to needles which were inserted into blood vessels in my feet. Sometimes at this stage someone would say a reassuring word to me at the beginning. This was one of those times.

Although I couldn't see any faces behind the green masks, their voices as they talked shop to each other always made me feel better. My life was literally in their hands so any encouragement I could give myself about them was a straw I readily grasped.

The operating rooms at Fitzsimmons were on the north side of the main hospital up on the third floor. I seem to remember a large plate glass window but the crowd of green gowns surrounded me so rapidly I never had time to study what I thought I was seeing. Besides, I was groggy from the prep shot.

Within a few minutes of being wheeled into the room and after the intravenous tubes were set up someone would say "Sodium Pentothal on."

"Okay, Lieutenant, start counting backward from ten," someone else would tell me.

I never remember counting more than a few numbers before I blacked out.

This skin-graft operation added new pain to my body. The skin removal from the top of my thighs was only a single layer thick, the same layer that peels off after a sunburn. I was told the process would leave no disfigurement. At the time I believed them. The thin net of cloth laid over the raw skin left behind slowly dried and peeled up at the edges as the skin was replaced.

It burned and itched like blazes but the skin did heal. However, a faint scar stayed, like a pale shadow, in the shape of long strips that had been cut away.

But the payoff was new skin over the raw tissue of my hand and arm. The fingers of the hand were curled in a stiff immovable claw and this new skin was supposed to free up the muscles and tendons so that physical therapists could work out the stiffness in my fingers.

One day infection hit. As I lay in the bed rocking from side to side with pain and fever, I got to feeling sorry for myself. I hated the dinks, the medical staff, myself, everyone I could think of. How much more could I take?

My body had been a battleground for too long.

Maybe if I could destroy something I would feel better. A thought came forth that the only thing I had any control over anymore was my mind, and I could will myself to destruction like some of the wounded I had seen in Vietnam. But a counterthought popped up and won out—that it would be an absurdity even to attempt that.

Sometimes a man has to be reminded to take each day by itself. If he gets to thinking about nothing but when he will be out of the hospital he will go crazy looking at that impossible amount of time in front of him. It was best to think only about today and tomorrow. Each day, for weeks, for months, I forced myself to think like that.

Patience was all. If I had been impatient before my wound, I learned in the hospital that patience could be developed. I had to learn to wait, to outlast the pain, to ignore the occasional pretentious, condescending, egocentric doctors, but most of all I learned not to accept defeat in any way, shape, or form.

One day Pam rolled my wheelchair out onto the balcony of Ward 5 West. She thought the sunshine would be good for me. She pointed out Denver to the west and the Rocky Mountains strung north to south in a long ragged line directly west of Denver's city limits. My geography was a little hazy. I thought California was right on the other side of the first mountain range.

Thinking of California made me remember good times with Bob Hutchinson. Bob and Benny Goodstone had been my OCS roommates at Fort Benning. Bob had become my best friend right before I had shipped out for Vietnam. I had visited him and his parents at their home in California, on my way to San Francisco. He was going over a few weeks after me and I knew he had been assigned to the Delta down south. That close to Saigon would be good duty. We had made a bet during a bit of infantry bravado as to which one of us would win the most medals and receive the most purple hearts.

After Pam returned me to my room I asked a Red Cross lady to write a letter for me to Bob telling him what had happened to me and that I had won the bet—all the beer I could drink in one night.

I felt happy after the Red Cross lady left. It would be good to hear from him. Maybe he would visit me when he got back from 'Nam.

"Hey, Lieutenant! There's a friend of yours out in the ward. He just came in a while ago on the Medivac," Pam called out.

"Who is it?"

"You've got to get up and go find out for yourself."

"Oh shit. Well, help me up."

Pam helped me out of bed and into my slippers. I shuffled into the ward with her help and was astonished to see Hank Jordan from Delta Company, who had been the leader of the Fourth Platoon. He was grinning broadly like a Cheshire cat. His left arm had been blown away too, leaving only about an eight-inch stump, one inch longer than mine.

"4–6, what the hell are you doing here?" I asked stupidly.

"The same thing you are, 1–6. How the hell are you?"

"Hey, I'm doing okay. What happened to you?"

"American artillery, 105s. We were on line to attack an enemy position and Delta 6 had called for artillery to soften them up. When they opened fire one of the guns wasn't sighted in properly and his shells landed right on top of us. Eight guys got hit—Spagg, your machine gunner, was one of them. By the way, I'm Delta 1–6 now. Sells had me take over your platoon after you got hit. It was our platoon that got hit. Christ, eight of us got it before we could get the guns to cease fire. It was a fucking mess. Nobody got killed though. I received the worst wound."

"Shit, two Delta 1–6s in a row got their left arms blown off. Whoever took over from you must be paranoid about left arms. What happened after I got hit?"

"Christ, I was with Captain Sells when Marley called and said you had been wounded real bad. Sells took off at a dead run to try and get to you before the dust-off got there. Your platoon was so shook up that he loggered them in (made camp) for the rest of the day until they settled down. He went in with Colonel Weir to see you the next day and when he came back he was pretty shaken. He said he never wanted to go into another ward like that in his life."

"God, my time perspective has been all screwed up ever since I was hit. I remember him and Colonel Weir being there but I thought a couple of days had passed at least."

"Well, right after I took over we continued to work that

area. It was pure hell. About a week later a dog team was assigned to the platoon to help us find dinks hiding in the tunnels. We captured one dink and he said he would lead us to an arms cache. None of the guys trusted the dink and a few thought we should go ahead and kill him, but the decision was to go ahead. . . .''

"Yeah," I interjected, "I saw Gary in the intensive care ward in the 85th Evac at Qui Nhon and he told me the dink led you into a booby trap!"

"We tried to get the dink but he got away. Not too long after that we were loggered in one night and we got mortared by the dinks. One of the shells dropped right in a foxhole and killed Doc, Idling, Robinson, and Murray. Then later on when the 105s hit us the First Platoon was down to nothing. January was a bad month for 1–6. The company had to be pulled out of the field because of all the casualties. It was a lick!"

I was stunned. My platoon, Hank's platoon, was gone, wiped out in a few weeks.

"What a fucking lick," I murmured. My men were gone.

My Wife's First Visit

A wound and pain are so absolutely dominating that they shut out the rest of life. I had not thought much of my wife, Linda, and our children since Vietnam. But now that I was inching back into the world, she reentered my thoughts. I was in fact afraid.

Hank Jordan's wife had unknowingly built my confidence to meet Linda. Hank could get around pretty well, so he had been spending a lot of time in my room. We were such friends that the nurses had arranged to put us in a double bedroom on 5 West, catty-corner from the nurses' station right across the hall from the debridement room. Since I had to go into that room twice a day, I wasn't crazy about being any closer to it, but sharing a room with someone to talk to was worth any price.

Hank's wife had recently moved out to Denver from their home near Chicago, into an apartment right outside the hospital grounds. Hank was very proud of her and, after we were introduced, I could see why.

Margaret was her name but she preferred to be called Molly and she was a beautiful lady in both spirit and body. She was about five feet six inches tall, slightly built, with light brown hair and green eyes. Molly taught elementary school, and she was teaching me again about men and women each time she came to see Hank. Perhaps that sort of love was possible for Linda and me.

In any case, all three of us were looking forward to Linda's visit. Hank, Molly, and I got along so well they believed and I hoped that Linda would fit right into our group.

It was morning. I lay propped up on pillows closely monitoring the traffic in the hall passing our door.

What would she look like? What do I look like? What will she think when she sees me? Oh, my God, I'm scared but I must act brave. Jesus, how will I make a living? How can I support a wife and a family? Do these bandages stink? Will she recognize me? What will I say to her?''

Finally, Linda came to the open door. The nurse who had led her there stuck her head in and cheerfully said, "Got a guest for you, Lieutenant Downs!"

Linda walked slowly into the room, stopping by my side, where we gazed at each other for a clumsy, embarrassing moment struggling for the right thing to say.

My mind registered at last—this woman is my wife and the mother of my daughter and stepdaughter.

Linda is tall, five feet eight inches, of medium build, with brown hair and hazel eyes. She was always fiercely protective of her children and all other matters involving her life, a no-nonsense, tough lady who had been knocked around in life but had survived.

The one word to describe her was "realistic." "How the hell did we end up together," I wondered. We must have loved each other. Now we have a daughter. I had spent our married life away from both of them. I had been in the army when I married Linda and from then on had been in various army bases being trained. We had decided she would not follow me around the camps so I rarely saw her except for the occasional trips home during leave.

When our daughter, Teri Jo, was born in St. Elizabeth's Hospital in Danville, Illinois, I was in OCS at Fort Benning Infantry School in Georgia. My company commander refused to grant me leave. Children, he said, are born all the time and there was nothing I could do even if I were there. Besides, there was a war on. The army needed second lieutenants.

I had been standing at attention in front of his desk while he explained his logic to me. Although standing at a good military brace, I was raging inside at the illogic of his explanation. I felt it was only right that I be at home for the birth of my first child, but it was not to be.

Well, what with one thing and another the army demanded and received most of my time, while Linda was left home to cope with raising two children and working to supplement the bit of pay (eighty-eight dollars a month at first) that I was sending home. Initially I kept five dollars for shaving lotion, razor blades, and small incidentals; later as I made more money I kept a little more but not much.

Finally, I was commissioned a second lieutenant, making three hundred sixty dollars a month and was stationed at Fort Gordon, Georgia, as a training officer. After a few months Linda loaded her 1961 Chevy with the two kids and our meager belongings and drove from Paris, Illinois, to Augusta, Georgia, where we lived outside the army base for a

few months. Just about the time we got used to living together as husband and wife and learned to cope with the
normal problems, I received orders for Vietnam.

I had hoped to receive orders for helicopter flight school
first, which would have meant another nine months in the
States. We could have lived together for those nine months,
but the orders for flight school arrived a week after the orders
for Vietnam. When I went to make my case before the battalion commander, he told me that orders for Vietnam
superseded orders for anything, so I would have to go to
Vietnam first. I could apply for flight school later.

Downcast, I returned to our sparse brick living quarters
and told Linda to pack up. In three weeks I was going to
'Nam.

When we left Fort Gordon, we drove all night and arrived
in Paris, Illinois, soon after daybreak.

After a week's leave, Linda and her sister and brother-
in-law drove me across Illinois to Scott Air Force Base outside of St. Louis.

At 1:00 A.M. on a muggy late August night, I pulled my
duffel bag out of the old Chevy, kissed Linda goodbye, and
went into the terminal to catch a military hop across country
to the army embarkation point at Oakland, California.

That was in August 1967. I left Linda sitting in the Chevy
in the parking lot next to the terminal building. Now it was
March 1968 and Linda had once again come to me, flying
one thousand miles to an army hospital in Aurora, Colorado,
just east of Denver.

I reckoned I hadn't provided her with much of a marriage
so far and she probably didn't figure on her odds improving
any with me wounded like this. However, she was the
mother of my child. I resolved to make a better home for
her and my daughter as soon as I got the chance.

But now I had to get through the next few minutes and

I couldn't think of anything clever to say. I was so happy to have her here, all I could blurt out was, "Hi, hon, it's good to see you!"

And Linda replied, "Hello, how are you doing?"

And so it went, not very well. When Linda left to return to the hospital hostel provided for out-of-town visitors, I felt uneasy. Our time together had not been comfortable.

The thing we really needed to talk about—the future— had not been discussed. Linda had spoken of her relatives and the two girls, of house repairs, the car's tune-up, even of the weather.

I had introduced Hank and Molly to Linda and they didn't seem to click, but I put that down to nervousness. I was making any excuse to stave off the inevitable.

As usual I spent a restless night, made worse than usual by the worry that another battle was forming in my future. But perhaps I was overdramatizing. After all, with no prep-aration, no guidance on what to say, no one to counsel her on what I had been through or what I needed now, Linda had walked in cold to a large army hospital to meet her one-armed, mutilated husband, who had himself received no counseling on what to do or to expect.

At times like these, I alternated between anger and out-right hate toward the chaplains, the psychologists, and all the other professionals who were supposed to deal with the problems of the spirit, the mind, and the soul.

Where the hell were these people? I knew where. The psychologists and psychiatrists on the base only worked with the psychotics who were sent to them. Neither I nor the other guys on the ward were psychotic, but we sure as hell did need counseling. I had things on my mind that needed an-swers.

And I damn sure wasn't going to go down to some shrink's office and ask for help. That kind of shit went into your medical records, and it stayed on your records forever. Talking among ourselves, we agreed that we didn't want to be considered crazy.

Because of her job and the two girls back in Paris, Illinois, Linda could stay only three days. She stood next to my bed while she explained why she had to leave. She was needed back home. The army was taking good care of me, I told her; no sweat.

Our moods reflected the melancholy we felt. She had mentioned during the visit that she had seen her ex-husband while I was in Vietnam. She hinted that she was still seeing him, but neither of us pursued the issue. We both wanted to avoid the truth. I looked up at her standing by my side and knew we were finished. However, we were inextricably tied together through our daughter, Teri Jo. Therefore, we would never be completely finished. She left.

"Perhaps I am wrong," I mused. "Yeah, that must be it. The drugs, my wounds, the shitty experience she has had to go through here in the hospital by seeing all of these wounded guys have combined to make her edgy and to increase my already heightened apprehension about my future.

"I can overcome this, just like everything else I have overcome since I have been wounded. I will do it! I will not be defeated! My daughter is at stake. I will not lose her. Goddamn it!" Then I faded.

I pulled the cocking lever back on my M-60 machine gun and released the lever, letting the spring push the bolt through the firing chamber where it smoothly snagged a 7.62 bullet from the belt of ammunition hanging from the left side of the gun. The bolt slid the round into the barrel, locking into place behind the bullet.

I was in full combat-web gear, standing in a sunny clearing backed by a jungle tree line wavering in the muggy air.

My helmet was off, lying on the ground next to my rucksack at my feet. I was holding the M-60 with both hands in a firing position at waist level, the weight of the gun supported by a makeshift sling attached to both ends of the gun and looped over my shoulder. The ammo belt hung down to the grass.

I sensed danger, felt a raging hatred at the complexities of the enemy out there, something I could not quite see. I stood alone in the clearing, struggling to make sense out of it, helpless and vulnerable because something beyond my control, something invisible, was having or going to have an influence on my life.

My fear flowed from a certainty that the force did not care about me. My anger resulted from my refusal to accept that. I would fight and win my point, regardless of the strength or power of that force.

I could win by reducing everything to one fact—me against the enemy, the way it was in the jungle. We survived by destroying.

I swung a bit to the left to bring an area near the tree line more into focus. I believe I saw her there. I fired a long burst toward her. The smell of cordite, the sound of stuttering explosions, the shuddering of my body as I wrestled with the M-60 to keep it pointed in the right direction, and the thin red streaks of tracer fire streaking into the tree line flicked through my consciousness.

I felt serene at the destruction I had wrought.

The Promotion

A short time later, we learned that the chief of staff for the army, General Harold K. Johnson, would visit the hospital, to make rounds and award some medals. The hospital staff needed to know who was eligible for medals, and it was discovered that I had four purple hearts coming, so I was one of those chosen to receive a purple heart with three oak-leaf clusters.

I had never met a general, let alone the chief of staff of the army. On the appointed day I was dressed in clean blue pajamas and a blue hospital robe, and as the general and his entourage neared our room Nurse Gish swung me up to sit on the edge of my bed. Hank and Molly were there, too.

When General Johnson entered the room, I was immediately struck by the fact that he looked like a nice old gentleman, very military in his bearing. An enormous mass of medals covered the left chest of his dress greens. One of the hospital staff introduced us. I could not salute or shake hands, but I smiled and he smiled back. For some reason I had not expected that a general would smile.

"So, Lieutenant Downs, you are the man who is to be awarded four purple hearts?"

"Yes, sir."

"That is quite an accomplishment. What outfit were you with?"

"Fourth Division, sir. Third Brigade, First of the Fourteenth, the Golden Dragons operating up in I Corps."

"Oh yes, that's Colonel Weir's outfit. A good man."

"Yes, sir. He came to visit me after I got hit."

"What happened to you, Lieutenant?"

"I stepped on a Bouncing Betty."

"You're very lucky to be here, son."

"Yes, sir, it could have been worse. I could have lost my legs and my right arm, or I could have been killed. I am lucky, all right."

"I am proud to award the purple heart with three oak-leaf clusters to you, Lieutenant Downs," he said, lifting the medal from its container held by an aide, and pinned it to my pajama top. The photographers' cameras flashed.

"Say, son, is there anything I can do for you?"

I caught my breath. This was unexpected, but there was something. I had been worried that the transfers from unit to hospitals had screwed up my records.

"Well, sir, all second lieutenants are supposed to be promoted after one year, and I haven't gotten my promotion yet."

General Johnson put his hand on my shoulder and looked into my eyes. "Lieutenant, from this moment on you are a first lieutenant." He turned to one of his staff. "Major, see that this young man is promoted immediately."

There was a flurry of activity as the photographers took more pictures and the major moved up to ask me the necessary questions about my serial number and so forth.

I was flabbergasted. I thought that the general would have someone check on it. I certainly never expected a four-star general to promote me on the spot.

Considering the maimed soldiers he had been visiting all day, promoting me to first lieutenant had probably been a real pleasure for him. At least he could give me something.

After the general left, the story of my request spread like wildfire through the hospital. It was generally agreed that I should have asked to be jumped to captain.

Physical Therapy

Hank and Molly had left. Linda was gone. The electricity generated by General Johnson had died. I was alone and that was good. I needed to think without interruption.

I had not really been analyzing that missing left arm. I had been concentrating on what I had left—the right arm and both legs. But now my brave front was crumbling. I was very, very worried about the consequences of losing an arm. And so high up, too; almost to the shoulder. I didn't want to think about it. Up to now, my other wounds had been painfully dominant. Except for phantom pain and healing pain, my stump had hurt the least of all.

When I tried to reach out my arms to Linda, the thought slammed home. I had been kidding myself. I must work much harder to regain the use of my right arm. And I didn't know what I could do with my stump. I had been exercising it regularly, rotating it in circles, first one direction and then another, because a physical therapist in the 85th Evac in Vietnam had recommended that. She said that a healthy stump would take a good-fitting prosthesis.

It had not been hard to avoid going down to the east wing on the first floor where physical therapy was located. But with my new awareness of the limitations in store for me if I didn't start a therapy program, I resolved to attend PT (physical therapy) and OT (occupational therapy) regularly.

I was really beginning to feel better, and I attributed this to the fact that the pain shots were six or eight hours apart, which allowed time for my brain to defog. Also, I could climb down from bed by myself and walk short distances. To be able to move about under my own steam did wonders for morale.

In line with my thinking about therapy, the doctors at the hand clinic asked for and received a reporting schedule for me to attend PT each day in order to build my muscles back to where they would function properly again. I also received instructions to start showing up for the regular sessions of OT.

They wanted me to start right away, so the next day I crept painfully down the hall of 5 West to the elevator bank. As I traveled the labyrinthine path of halls, elevators, and doorways to PT, I felt pretty sorry for myself.

My legs had tightened up from the weeks of inactivity, and from the shrapnel having torn out chunks of muscle, ligament, and tissue. It seemed everything added to my miseries.

I shuffled along bent like an old man I had once seen back in Indiana. A friend and I had driven over to Terre Haute and, while waiting at a stop light on Wabash Avenue, I had watched an old man crossing in front of my 1956 Ford. He was so bent over that the upper part of his body angled ninety degrees to the ground. The friend with me answered my unspoken question by saying that the old man had probably been a local coal miner. After a lifetime of working stooped over in the mines, their spines were permanently ruined. Now as I shuffled along the hospital corridors I thought of that old man crossing the street in the bright Indiana sun.

"All right, get your ass in gear, Downs," I mumbled to myself.

I went through a door into a large waiting room and on to the clerk working on a ledger, to report myself present. She wrote my name, rank, serial number, and room number down in her book and directed me through a set of double doors.

The physical therapy clinic was a clinic of pain. The kind of pain that comes from stretching muscles and tendons just a little bit farther than they were used to stretching the day before. When men were assigned to the physical therapy clinic it was because they were healing, and if men were in good enough shape to heal, they were in good enough shape to bitch. There were plenty of groans and gritted teeth to prove that.

That first day at PT I saw things I had never seen before. Legless men or men with leg injuries lay on mats on the floor as kneeling PT nurses or orderlies held stumps or maimed legs in their hands forcing them back into the angles they once had assumed so naturally. Hip joints, knee joints, all being made to bend, to rotate, to stretch. Men with maimed arms and hands sat patiently as their elbow, shoulder, wrist, and finger joints were bent painfully into positions that would one day be natural again. Men whose bodies were paralyzed from spinal injuries stoically lay staring at the ceiling or at their therapists as their bodies were moved painlessly from one position to another. There were high spirits among the staff and patients as groans were interspersed with kidding and laughter.

Everywhere I looked I saw someone who was in worse shape than I. The chief nurse, a major, introduced herself and the staff as she led me back to her workroom.

I had on blue hospital pajamas, white cotton slippers, and a robe. I was cold all the time so I wore a robe everywhere. She removed my robe and helped me to sit down. Then she started examining my legs, gently testing them for flexibility as she kept up a constant friendly chatter about what she was doing.

Jesus, it hurt! But this was no place to be a crybaby; guys in worse shape than I were taking their therapy in stride, trying their best to accomplish what they could with what they had.

One man sitting next to me had been holding a mortar shell in his hands when it had prematurely exploded. There had been enough left of his hands that the surgeons had been able to cut back through his palms and fuse his finger bones together so that he now had two hands that looked and operated like lobster claws. After the initial shock at seeing this I realized that he was able to use his two hands for everything even though they had, at first sight, looked gruesome.

To me, to all of us, the grotesque was becoming commonplace, and if the malformed limb was functional, grotesque became secondary. We didn't care much what it looked like, as long as it worked. We were thankful to have anything left to work with.

After finishing a conversation with the soldier who had claw hands, I turned my attention to the major. She had finished examining my legs and now put me into a sitting position next to a table and rested my arm upon its cold surface.

All sounds from the room fled from my mind as I stared at my claw hand. Nothing else mattered or could intrude into the unspoken fear that had been building since the first week of March.

That had been when my arm was covered with skin grafts from my leg. The skin grafts had taken, which facilitated the healing of the arm because it now had a natural protective covering. However, as the skin grafts had adhered to the underlying tissues, muscles, and tendons, my hand had drawn up into a nonfunctional claw. The nerve damage was still unknown. There was a faint sense of feeling in my little finger. At least now when I ate I could hold a fork between my little finger and the finger next to it by having a nurse tape them together. Otherwise, I was limited to mass movements of the arm.

I had no idea what to hope for. I closely watched the major's expression for an indication.

My hand was lying on its back, each finger curled into its own crooked pattern, depending on the underlying muscle, tendon, and nerve damage.

The major took my fingers and slowly tried to straighten them. She alternately watched my hand and my eyes as she did this. I grimaced and rose from the chair as she pulled a finger down.

"I'm sorry, Lieutenant, but these digits have not moved in a long time. We are going to have to work very hard in order for you to recover function in them."

"They're going to work, though, huh?" I asked eagerly. "You don't think there's too much damage?"

"No, I didn't say that. I said we had a lot of work ahead of us. We'll know better in a week or so what this hand can do later on. Just don't miss any of my sessions and we'll get along fine." She smiled as she bent another finger a fraction of an inch. It hurt so deeply up the length of my arm, it felt as if a sliver of fire was burning under the flesh.

But I was overjoyed to feel the pain. The nerves were at least partially intact.

The major worked away, now slightly bending, slightly twisting, kneading, forcing, always gently. After about thirty minutes I had to cry "uncle." Sweat was beaded on my forehead and body. The major had brought tears to my eyes from the efforts to bend my fingers. It felt so good when she stopped that I almost laughed out loud in relief.

She set up an appointment for me with the orthotic laboratory and took me over to the building behind the main hospital where the lab was located. The orthodist built a frame which fit over the back of my hand and forearm. Dangling by rubber bands from the frame were five small leather pouches. The idea was to fit each finger into a pouch so a steady pressure from the rubber bands would pull up on the fingers, slowly straightening them out of the claw position.

That device was one painful son of a bitch. I was supposed to wear it day and night, but I simply could not bear the dull, throbbing ache it sent through my hand, arm, and shoulder.

After a week of worse nights than usual, I decided not to wear it while trying to sleep.

Occupational Therapy

Physical therapy is the treatment of injury by physical means like exercise, whereas occupational therapy is done by means of work in the arts and crafts. I didn't want to go to OT but after the major got me fixed up with the hand brace she pushed me into it. She also gave me a small pillow to carry around so I would have something to pad my ass when I sat down. Another reason I did not want to go was because I had heard about the kindergarten tasks they put one to work on. The really big deal in OT was rug weaving. Somehow or another it did not seem right for an adult male to be making pot holders either, but they had a setup for those.

As I moped down the hall toward OT I schemed how I would escape this clinic first chance I got.

I turned the corner to the hall outside the OT clinic. Seeing the young men lined up along both sides of the hall caused me to flush in embarrassment at my selfish thoughts of a moment ago. Men with every imaginable wound were laughing and talking animatedly with each other as they waited for the OT clinics to open. Men with no legs balanced on the back two legs of their wheelchairs as they pirouetted around each other; a man with no arms was accepting a light for his cigarette from a man with one arm; a blind man was listening intently to the description of his surroundings from a man who was horribly scarred from burn wounds; two men missing large sections of skull were being led to chairs by men on crutches. . . . the sight of these blue-robed, band-aged and damaged men enjoying the camaraderie of each other raised my spirits. I was glad to be among a group of men again who were enjoying life.

I put my pillow down and sat on a vacant chair next to a man who had a hook sticking out of one sleeve. He offered me a cigarette and when I said yes he reached into his robe chest pocket with his hook and pulled out a package. He then shook one out and stuck it in my lips.

"Can't use your hand yet with that fucking contraption on there, can you?" He gestured with his hook toward my hand brace.

"Naw, about the only thing I can do is scratch my nose. They can't figure out what the son of a bitch is going to be good for whenever it heals up."

"Hell's bells, as long as you can drink beer and hold your dick, that's all you need anyhow." We both laughed at this version of the often-repeated line.

"Yeah, no shit . . . Say, how does that hook work, anyway? They've been talking about putting an arm on me but I don't know a Goddamn thing about it. The only hooks I ever saw were on men back home in Indiana whose hands had gotten caught in corn pickers, but I never asked them about their hooks. I think I was afraid of hurting their feelings or something."

"Works easy; here, let me show you how I can light your cigarette using it."

He reached the hook into his robe pocket and withdrew a book of matches. He transferred this to his hand. He deftly pulled a match from the book with his hook and struck the match against the abrasive strip along the bottom of the matchbook, held immobile in the hand. He lifted his arm, and the burning match in the hook, up to my cigarette. I leaned forward and lit the Camel. He puffed the match out and held it over a butt-can where he opened the hook allowing the match to fall.

I was impressed. He had accomplished with his hook a chore so simple that ordinary people didn't have to think about it, and yet it required a dexterity absolutely beyond my imagination.

Immediately I saw that the hook represented independence and freedom. However, it looked sinister.

I moved my stump up and looked at the Ace bandage wrapped tightly around it.

"You know . . . I got to get one of those things."

"Fuckin' A. Just tell the captain in charge of the OT clinic and she'll hustle you right over to the shop. They have one behind the main hospital somewhere close to where that brace was made."

* * *

When the clinic opened the men flooded into the rooms and sat down to the projects they had been working on.

Blind men were working on clay sculpture; men with damaged arms were painting—some by holding the brush in their teeth; the men with hooks were practicing picking up differently shaped pegs and inserting them into the appropriate holes; the men in wheelchairs were working on weaving; and a brain-injured soldier was working on staining glass.

Not only was the therapy supposed to be good for us by building our confidence in relearning how to get our basic motor skills back, but the sessions in OT helped to pass the time. It was a good social time.

A large part of the success of PT or OT was the great people who worked there. A robust cheerful blond captain was in charge of OT and her bouncing energy kept the whole place charged up. She was enthusiastic about everything and supportive of every one of her patients. No achievement by any of us was so minor she didn't reward us with a smile and words of further encouragement.

All of the people who worked there seemed to be of like temperament. It was a good thing, because some days a man would be so depressed he would take it out on the staff. They always seemed to take any abuse in stride and bounce right back until the man either got cheered up or left to go sulk in his bed.

The captain introduced herself and her staff and then pondered what I could do.

"How about painting, Lieutenant? We can fix up a set of brushes you can hold in your teeth. . . ."

"No. I'm not going to hold a paintbrush in my teeth. I couldn't paint a picture when I had two hands, let alone no hands."

"Let's see . . . let's try and start with . . . stained glass?" She looked at me hopefully.

I looked over at the brain-injured man concentrating on

the colored jagged pieces of glass. "Nope, can't handle that either."

"Well, you aren't getting out of here until you do something. Hmmm." She looked at the tips of my fingers sticking through the bandages. "Who cuts your nails?"

"The Red Cross lady."

"Well, I have an idea."

She rigged up a fingernail clipper fastened onto a board and jerry-built an extention onto one end of the clipper. She taught me to use my stump to press down on the extension.

For the first time I was able to do personal hygiene for myself.

After thirty minutes of hard work I managed to trim all five of my nails. I felt proud of myself and was glad she had persevered over my stubbornness.

There were times when I had to be forced to do something for my own good, especially in rehabilitation therapy. Progress was so slow it almost didn't seem worth it.

The captain came over to congratulate me and tell me that tomorrow she would take me over to the prosthesis shop to be fitted with an arm.

Surprisingly I did not like that idea. In spite of my earlier daydream about a hook, I was getting used to having one arm and I abhorred the idea of that alien plastic and metal device hanging from me, and I told the captain so.

"Now, Lieutenant, you'll be able to do so much more with a hook that you'll surprise yourself. Look at Johnson over there," she said, pointing to a black guy working at the shaped block board. He was sweating as he tried to pick up the differently shaped blocks with his hook to put them into the holes in the board.

"You'll be able to do that in no time," she assured me.

"I can't wait," I sourly assured her. "There is a big demand for guys who can put square pegs in square holes."

"I'm glad to see you are excited about it, Lieutenant, so

I'll be waiting tomorrow morning to get you fitted up," she smiled. "Right?"

"Right," I reluctantly answered. "I'll be here."

The Arm

The next morning she was smiling and she had not, as I had hoped, forgotten where we were going. She and an orderly took me through an underground tunnel to an adjoining building where the prosthesis shop was located. The tunnel floor was covered with water so I was forced to walk along a narrow ledge along the wall that was a few inches higher than the floor so my cloth slippers would not get soaked. She put her arm around me to help me maintain balance on the narrow ledge and cheerfully trudged through the water joking with me and the orderly. I wondered if she ever had a bad day.

As I jostled next to her I began to notice the smell of her perfume and take notice of her body rubbing against me. I also became aware of another sensation I had not felt since I had been wounded. I was embarrassed but she just laughed.

"At least that land mine didn't blow everything to pieces, Lieutenant."

I felt a flush rushing up my neck and across my face and looked at the orderly who was discreetly walking far ahead of us. Although I was very embarrassed I was also relieved because I had not been sure if my internal injuries had ruined me or not.

"Christ, what a time to discuss this," I murmured as I tried to step gingerly along the ledge.

"Maybe this trip to the prosthesis shop won't be so bad after all," I joked with her as my spirits rose in concert with my body.

I was almost sorry to reach the end of the flooded area.

With a different outlook on life, I was very interested in the prosthesis shop as we entered through the doorway. A specialist E-5 walked up to us and introduced himself as he guided me to a chair.

"Welcome to the best limb shop in the army, Lieutenant. We'll fix you up with a temporary arm that will work almost as good as your real one," he assured me. "First we'll have to take a cast so we can fit you properly."

As he busied himself preparing for the fitting I looked at the shop.

In order to fabricate the artificial limbs intimately to the human body I guess I had expected bright, shiny, esoteric machines something like the instruments used by surgeons.

What I saw was a machine shop. Some of these tools must have weighed a quarter of a ton. There was a drill press, belt sander, grinder, band saw, lathe, vise, sewing machine, and other tools I wasn't sure of as to function. Each one stood by itself in a line along the wall or down the middle of the well-lit room. There was ample work space around each of the free-standing machines.

A smell of leather, machine oil, glue, plastics, resins, and wood shavings permeated the air.

Sounds fluctuated in teeth-gritting shrieks as a particular material was pushed into the cutting teeth on the band saw. The other sounds from the machinery in use were loud but no one seemed to notice but me. Someone was hammering in the background.

The workers wore white aprons with large waist pockets. Stacked or hung here and there throughout the shop were the fruits of their labor.

On one workbench were black shoes modified to hold a brace of two metal rods inserted into the heel and running about halfway up the calf.

Dozens of artificial feet stood on one table; hollow legs of various sizes and lengths for different levels of amputation

were leaning in corners. Their naked mannequin shiny plastic
flesh tried miserably to imitate the human limb, but to my
eye seemed only to accentuate their falseness. A few arms
hung on the wall and I fixed on them. They looked horrible
to me.

How could I wear so much ugly metal and plastic and a
harness to hold it onto me? How could I go out into public
in that thing? Everyone would stare at me like I was some
kind of freak. That alien thing was not going to replace my
flesh. Why pretend? I didn't want attention drawn to my miss-
ing arm. I could hide it easier by folding up an empty sleeve.

I was used to the idea of doing without an arm. But to
have to go through the rest of my life without an arm . . .
I wanted to puke just thinking about spending forty or fifty
years without being able to clap my hands, or twiddle my
thumbs, or crack my knuckles, or learn to play the guitar,
or hold a baby, or do pushups, or rub my hands together
for warmth, or use both hands to make love.

I loved my hand and my arm and now they were cremated
in Vietnam. I wanted to scream it to the world. But I didn't.

Instead, I looked up morosely at the captain standing next
to my chair. She, unaware of the turmoil in me, was watching with interest one of the men working at a machine making
a leg.

"I'm not going to wear the son of a bitch," I murmured.
But as soon as I said it, a flash of insight made me think I
was wrong. I was giving up and that just wasn't my style.

She looked down at me in surprise, her smile replaced by
concern.

"What? What did you say, Lieutenant?"

I looked up at her guiltily. "Uh, uh. . . . I said I'm going
to wear the son of a bitch."

"That's good, but I do wish you men didn't swear so much."

"Yes, ma'am."

The specialist finished stirring the concoction he had mixed together. He wiped his hands clean with a rag and picked up the container with his left hand and with his right hand picked up an arm lying on the workbench nearby.

As he came toward me I could not take my eyes off the arm—my mouth felt cotton-dry, my lower jaw was jutting out, my teeth were clamped together, and my stomach was doing flip-flops. I was trying to keep my feelings hidden because I did not want to appear weak or crybabyish, but inside my guts were tied up in knots. I felt just like I did on a helicopter combat assault—scared to death but committed and determined to see it through.

He and the captain stood me up. The captain earlier had helped me remove my pajama top so my upper torso was naked. The specialist asked the captain to hold the arm in its natural position against my body and told me to insert my stump into the hollow top half of the upper arm. This particular arm was deliberately too large for me because he was going to pour the liquid he had just mixed into it around my stump. The liquid would quickly solidify and form a mold of my stump. He would then remove the arm, slide the mold from my stump and fashion a custom-made arm using the mold as a model.

He said he could not wait any longer or the stuff would solidify and for me to hold still. He asked me to keep my stump in the middle so the liquid would flow evenly around it. I nodded dumbly as he poured the liquid. It was warm and smelled like latex, but there was no pain.

After a few minutes he removed the arm and took out the mold. He then measured the length of my other arm from shoulder to elbow, and elbow to wrist, writing the figures on a slip of paper.

As he did that I studied and mused about the arm leaning where he had put it against the chair. It had not been so bad. It made me feel creepy and I had not liked the feel of the thing against my skin, but this thing was going to be a part of my life as long as I lived.

This is the way it looked to me that day and this is the way it would be:

It looked like a complete arm. There was the upper arm, the elbow joint, the forearm, and a hook. At the top of the upper arm was fastened a harness that held the arm onto the body. The harness was shaped roughly like a figure eight. It was made of nylon straps and had two or three adjustable buckles. Both the upper and lower arm were hollow for lightness.

To wear it, the stump slipped into the hollow upper arm. The harness criss-crossed my back and the opposite loop of the figure-eight harness went over the other arm, up under the armpit. The harness was adjusted until it was snug across the back of the shoulder. This allowed the weight of the artificial arm to be held in place and the strain to be taken by the upper shoulder muscle and opposite arm. The arm and harness could be shrugged on and off in seconds.

Sewed to the harness in back was a cable which ran along the upper portion of the arm, down along the lower arm, ending in a tiny ball-bearing which rested in a socket at the end of a short, one-inch lever jutting out from the hook where the thumb would have been.

The hook was not a single piece of metal like Captain Hook's or a farmer's hay hook. This hook opened. Where the wrist would have been was a ball-bearing joint from which stemmed two hook-shaped pieces of metal side by side. One side was fixed solidly at the wrist joint and the other side could be rotated in a short arc. The lever or thumb jutted from the movable side.

Located directly in front of the juncture where the two rotated was a minor indentation which held thick rubber bands. They were about where the middle of the hand would have been (back and palm) and they held the two hooks together.

The harness fit snugly enough that when the shoulder blades were spread apart, the tension on the harness would pull the cable which in turn would pull the lever forcing one side of the hook away from the immovable side of the hook. As the shoulder muscles relaxed, the tension was eased off the cable and the rubber bands squeezed the two halves of the hook together.

The strength of the hook's grip depended on how many rubber bands a man wanted to wear. At first we used to show off by putting on so many we could crush beer glasses whenever we went to the bars outside the hospital. But for practicability we ended up putting on just enough rubber bands so we could open the hook without bunching up our shoulder muscles like King Kong.

The elbow joint had to be locked before the hook could be opened because the same cable and shoulder muscles moved the forearm up and down when the elbow joint was unlocked. Another cable was used to lock and unlock the elbow. This cable was sewed to the harness where it came over the top of the shoulder, and it was fastened to a small lever within the elbow mechanism. By shrugging down and backward with the shoulder on the side with the stump the tension on the cable would move it up a tad, moving the small lever which rotated a little device that locked on one pull of the cable and unlocked on the next pull. There were about eleven different positions in which the elbow could be locked. This range was from full extension of the arm to folding it up almost double.

When the arm is folded the hook is level with my face. This caused a problem when I was learning to use the arm because the same cable which opens the hook when the elbow is locked is the same cable which lifts the forearm when the elbow is unlocked.

Before I learned to "sense" whether the elbow was locked or not I would spread my shoulder blades to open the hook, thinking the elbow was locked. It would not be and the forearm would fly upward throwing the hook into my face. I chipped three teeth and banged myself on the chin and face numerous times before I learned how to control the movement.

Once I finally received my arm, it would take only a few hours to get the hang of how it worked and two weeks before I felt proficient. Mistakes would continue to happen, like the day I was lying on my back in bed and lifted the arm straight up from my side. I was beginning to feel good about the arm and was idly examining it while the arm was almost straight above me, but it passed a critical angle and the forearm dropped from the force of gravity right into my lip and front tooth. I jumped out of bed spitting blood and pieces of tooth out onto the floor. It was only a tool and so had to be treated with caution.

Strangely enough I never developed any passion for this piece of machinery that is so intimately a part of my body. Cars have souls, trucks have characters, aircraft are spiritual, and ships have dignity. But the arm was just a tool to me without heart, spirit, or soul. Pride comes to me from my ability to use it effectively and the wonderment it generates in people's curiosity about how it works.

The arm gives me enjoyment and peace of mind because it not only functions well as an arm but is an asset when I am around people because they seem to receive pleasure from seeing how well I can use it. I never consider myself handicapped and neither do they. The artificial arm made this possible.

But I never imagined the future would be so good on that

day long ago with the specialist and the captain in the limbs shop at Fitzsimmons Army Hospital as I stood half-naked, scared, and hurting from the pain of my healing wounds.

After all the measurements were finished the captain led me back through the tunnel to the OT clinic. She explained that a private business, Long's Limb Shop, down on Colfax Avenue, had an army contract to fabricate the limbs. They would use the mold and measurements just taken and I would have to make two or three trips there for custom fitting before it was completed. Until then I could use a spare arm in the shop to practice with. I said that I would start practicing right away.

"I expect to see you tomorrow and I know you won't disappoint me, will you, Lieutenant?" She gave me one of her captain stares.

"You're Number One, Captain," I laughed, giving her the best compliment a soldier could give.

Little did we know I was scheduled for another operation. I would not be back for some time because the doctors were worried about the skin graft operation. It had not worked the way they had planned.

Old Friends, Family, and Volunteers

Other than the hospital staff there were three main categories of people who helped us readjust to the world. Old friends, family, and volunteers. In their own ways they helped to bring us back. The word had gone out from my family—I had been wounded in Vietnam and was now at the army hospital in Denver.

Judy Davan stopped by to visit. She lived in Denver and worked as a nurse. She was about my age and was from Covington, Indiana. Her mom belonged to the same church as my Grandma Ferguson, mom's mother. Grandma Fer-

guson had told Mrs. Davan, who had called Judy and told
her to stop by. She later sneaked a bottle of champagne into
my room when I got well enough to enjoy it. She also took
me to a couple of movies.

Uncle Marvin, my dad's oldest brother, drove my
Grandma Downs one thousand miles nonstop from their
farms near Hillsboro, Indiana. They visited for three days
and Uncle Marvin drove Grandma the thousand miles nonstop back home. Their visit was very special to me and bol-
stered my spirits more than any other single thing since I had
been wounded. I had spent a lot of time on their farms and
they were close family. It's where I would go when I left
here.

My second cousin, Andy Anderson, came with his wife,
Marge, and two of their children. Andy had left home in
Clinton, Indiana, in 1948, to visit Denver and had never gone
back. I had never met them but they now visited me regularly,
brought me a radio to put on my night stand, and when I got
better took me out to their home for Sunday dinner. I met
Susie, their oldest daughter, and her husband, Tom. Later,
Andy would assist me in getting accepted at the University
of Denver.

Dad and my sister, Pam, flew out to visit. Dad had had
a stroke and was not in such good shape himself. Pam had
come along to watch after him. Mom stayed home as she
had to work but she had written so I understood. She was
the only one working and times were hard back home.

Don Kessler, a friend of Dad's from Marshall, Illinois,
had moved from Marshall to Denver and he visited one night.
He had become very religious since moving to Denver, was
a Baptist, I think. At the end of each visit he would get down
on his knees and start praying in a loud voice for me and
the other "boys" in the ward. Some of the "boys" would
hear the commotion and come down the hall to stand outside

my room and watch the lieutenant get prayed over. Don also brought me a radio.

Other people I did not know but who had been friends of Dad or Mom from the old days would stop in to introduce themselves. Everyone who visited brought in a little piece of the world outside.

All these visits were morale builders and helped me to prepare for the day when I would finally leave the hospital to go home.

To complement visits by family and friends were the many people who provided individual volunteer services to the hospital or who were sponsored by groups to entertain us.

The Red Cross, Gray Ladies, and Candy Stripers did everything from pushing the library cart, cutting fingernails, escorting us when we needed help ambulating in wheelchairs, shampooing hair, writing letters, brushing teeth to other personal chores like tidying up our bed stands, or going to the P.X. to purchase magazines or cigarettes or whatever. For someone like me who could not use his hands they were a Godsend for the hundred and one little things I needed to do but could not.

The USO sponsored groups who came through the wards on a regular basis as they traveled from hospital to hospital. They would usually set up in the large open ward in the afternoon and we would gather around in our wheelchairs, sit on regular chairs or on the beds, or stand and watch the groups sing, dance, present a play, or perform whatever their speciality was.

Special groups composed of local people usually came out during the evening to entertain us in their way.

One group I particularly remember was the Playboy bunnies from the Denver Playboy Club. What a night! We had been informed earlier in the day that they were going to visit that night. All other subjects of conversation disappeared.

We did not know what the bunnies would do but we had a hell of a time speculating about it. Most of the guys were not old enough to get into a Playboy Club, let alone afford a key.

We made sure we were shaved and had on clean blue pajamas and robes when they arrived.

When they came into the ward shortly after supper, they were everything we had imagined. They had on black mini-skirts and tight white blouses. They had brought cookies and were dispensing them to the troops. When one of them came into my room and found I could not use my hand, she fed me a cookie by holding it while I ate it, tiny bite by tiny bite. My eyes about bugged out looking at her cleavage. She spread the word about the soldier who could not use his hand and different bunnies kept rotating through my room to feed me cookies.

Normally I did not like cookies, but I must have eaten two dozen that night.

Another night we were visited by the American Legion Post and their wives. They brought us hamburgers and fries from a fast-food chain. As soon as they came through the swinging doors into our ward we could smell the hamburgers and fries. My mouth started watering and when one of the American Legion guys came into the room he and his wife took it as their right to help feed me. I loved hamburgers and kept asking for more. They were astounded at the number I was putting down. He kept hollering out the door to bring in another one. He would stand there shaking his head ev-erytime he pushed another one into my mouth. With each shake of his head his garrison cap, festooned with conven-tion medals, would shine and twinkle.

After hospital food the taste of a hamburger was heaven, but the rich food did not set well with me. Later in the night I threw it all up.

And there were the people who just took it upon themselves to visit the hospital and do what they could to cheer us up.

My favorite was the old lady from Colorado Springs who rode the bus into Denver every Wednesday morning. She was short and a little heavyset. She always dressed up in bright colors, wore a hat, and had red rouge on her cheeks. She had a nervous twitch which shook her head slightly as she talked. She would spend about five minutes with each man and then move on. At the end of the day she rode the bus back to Colorado Springs. She had lost her husband in World War II and her only son in Korea. She always told us she was grateful to God we had made it back home. She was happy for us.

Benny Goodstone

Each day I walked down the hall I always checked to see who had just arrived. Hank had found me and I had found Gary. He had left the 85th Evac shortly after I, he said, and had gone to Japan.

There was the day I found one of the sergeants who had taken us through basic training when I entered the army. I thought he had been in the service for ten years the way he strutted around in his "Smoky Bear" hat, scaring us trainees half to death. His leg had been blown off below the knee. I saw by his card that he was younger than I was—only twenty-two.

I wondered how some of my friends were faring in the war. A lot of my OCS classmates had been wounded or killed. It all seemed so unreal somehow—those good men destroyed.

One day I stopped suddenly—shocked at the name I saw on the door jamb—GOODSTONE.

I had had two roommates at OCS. One was Bob Hutchinson, whom I had written to earlier, and the other was Benny Goodstone, a hardheaded kid from Wisconsin who talked forever about home.

I looked into the dark hospital room and wondered why the lights were turned off in the middle of the day. Was the still form lying on the hospital bed the same Benny Goodstone I knew?

"Hey, Benny, Benny Goodstone, are you awake?"

The figure on the bed lifted his head. "Yeah, who's there? Who is it?"

"It's Candidate Downs," I answered.

Switching on the light as I entered the room my heart swelled with the memory of our times together as roommates at OCS.

For a brief moment relief swept through me. Benny looked okay. But as I strode to his bedside, the scar tissue around his face and his staring eyes hit me with the sickening realization that Benny was blind. Also, there was a large dent in his forehead indicating that a piece of his skull was missing. When he pushed himself up to a sitting position, I noticed that his right hand was missing at the wrist.

Benny stared through me with sightless eyes. "Fred, Fred Downs, is that you?" His face broke into a smile and he reached out with his good hand.

I clasped it with my good hand and we pulled ourselves together. He reached up with his stump to lay it on my shoulder. His head rested on my chest as I breathed into his hair. "Yeah, Benny, it's me." We held each other for a few moments before I stepped back. "Hey man, it's good to see you. What happened to you anyway?"

"I'm not sure, Fred. The only thing I remember is that I was trying to dismantle a booby trap, some kind of grenade I think, and then I don't remember anything else."

"It looks like it went off in your face. You were probably fucking with something you weren't supposed to, as usual.

Didn't you have an engineer attached to your platoon to do that kind of shit?'' I admonished him.

''Yeah, but he was doing something else and I didn't want to wait on him. Besides, it looked simple so I thought I could handle it.''

''Just like that class on land-mine warfare at Fort Benning, huh? Remember Zorn was trying to dismantle that anti-tank mine? He was shaking so bad he set off the simulated charge and theoretically destroyed his whole team. We kidded him about that for days. Old Fisher would yell 'Bang!' everytime he saw Zorn.''

''And Zorn's blood pressure would shoot up until we thought he would explode without the help of a land mine.''

We laughed at the memory. Right before graduation the company commander had called us together to read off what branch we would be assigned to. Most of us were assigned to the infantry and Zorn had wanted the administration branch so badly that by the time Captain Cosand reached his name alphabetically, he was a nervous wreck. We were laying bets as to whether he would faint before his name was reached. When Captain Cosand read out that Zorn was assigned to administration he almost passed out from relief.

Yes, we were virile young men, cocky and sure of our destiny as great leaders on the battlefield. We disdained anyone who did not want to share in that glory. Zorn's foresight was greater than ours but we did not recognize it at that time.

Of the men from my OCS class assigned to the infantry, little did we know that our casualty rate of wounded and dead would be seventy to eighty percent. We were gung ho, invincible—such numbers were not within our comprehension.

If we had known what the casualty rate was going to be we would have accepted it as a matter of pride to be part of a group on the ''cutting edge'' of the fighting.

Our training had been intense and very good but we had

been playing at fighting and our dead were resurrected after each exercise. Being dead was unthinkable. A wound would be clean if we happened to get hit.

Looking into Benny's sightless eyes I thought how foolish we had been to believe such a thing.

"Fred, what happened to you? Are you hurt bad?"

"I stepped on a Bouncing Betty and blew my left arm off about six inches from the shoulder. Here you can feel the stump." I guided his hand to my arm and let him feel the bandaged end. He gently used his fingers to trace out the damage.

"I also about lost my right arm and both my legs but I think I am out of danger now. The only worry is how much function they can restore to my arms and legs. I fucked up, too, Benny," I ruefully commented.

"What about Bob, Fred? I heard he was down in the Delta."

"I don't know but I wrote to him a couple of weeks or so ago. At least the Red Cross lady wrote for me. I can't use my hand yet. I ought to hear from him pretty soon. Hey, what division were you with? I was with the Fourth Division, Third Brigade, First of the Fourteenth up in I Corps. It was bad up there I'll tell you. The dinks controlled everything we weren't standing on."

"The First Division: Big Red One," Benny proudly stated; "The Bloody One." He was referring to the arm patch which was a large number one in red against a green background. The casualty rate in the division had earned them the dubious distinction of living up to their patch, "The Bloody One," or perhaps it referred to all the enemy soldiers they had killed. It did not make much difference which way you believed, I guessed. A lot of men had died either way.

"You were with the Fourth Division? That's the arm patch with four ivy leaves, isn't it?"

"Yeah, we were known as the 'Fighting Ivy,' although

we preferred 'The Fighting Fourth,' but no one used anything but the 'Fighting Ivy.' It sounds more like a college football cheer than an infantry outfit, but we put in a good accounting of ourselves," I proudly reminded him.

Benny told me all about the motorcycle he had bought after OCS. He said he was the only lieutenant who rode to work on a motorcycle. When he got orders for Vietnam he had stored it away to use when he got back but now he guessed he would give it to one of his family.

We talked on and on but finally we were both too tired to go any further. We said goodbye and I promised to visit every day. I told him I was just across the hall so to holler if he needed anything.

At the doorway I turned to say goodbye once again. I saw a man I had lived with lying on a bed staring through darkness at the ceiling.

"See you later, huh Benny?"

"Yeah, Fred, I'll see you," he wearily replied.

"Fred."

"Yeah?"

"What happens now?"

"I don't know, Benny. They didn't prepare us for this."

"Yeah, but they should tell us now shouldn't they?"

"Well, they will, they will. There are all kinds of stuff to help us. I saw the prosthesis shop and there are all kinds of things they build to put us together again. Wait until you meet the captain in charge of OT. The Blonde Bombshell will get you rolling again. Don't worry, okay? Things will work out."

"Okay."

"I'll take up a collection and get you a tin cup. Hell, the guys on the ward will all chip in," I joked. "There's something for all of us to do. There's a guy over in 5 East with no arms or legs and we figure he can get a job as a base in a ballpark, and when I get my hook I'll play basketball. I'll have a hell of a hook shot."

Benny started to pick up on our humor. "I could get a job as a referee. Shit, those guys are blind anyway."

"Sure, there are enough of us on this ward that if we pool all our parts we should be able to make it. I'll provide the good looks, of course."

"Anybody as ugly as you used to be must be kidding himself. Did you get a head wound too?" he laughed.

Our humor was not so humorous, I guess, but it was all we had and we used it. Benny was smiling now and that was something.

"I'll go start that collection. See you tomorrow."

"Roger, Candidate Downs."

The Pedicle Graft

Despite all the efforts of bending and straining in PT my hand was frozen into a claw. All of the skin grafts the surgeons had put on my arm from wrist to elbow had adhered to the underlying muscles and tendons and had immobilized them.

After much deliberation and discussion during the last week of March, the surgeons in hand clinic decided that there was no recourse but more surgery. They told me they would replace the skin grafts on the forearm with a pedicle graft from my stomach.

I was dismayed at this news. Lately I had been going through a lot of minor surgery with the idea that the "cutting" was about finished. I figured once the operations stopped, the healing would speed up. I had to get out of here. I was beginning to be afraid of leaving the hospital. I was protected here plus I realized I was very dependent still upon the pain-killing drugs. So dependent, in fact, that I had made friends with a nurse who was hooked herself and was snitching the "shit" on the side. She would come into my room and give me a "special" shot which was much stronger than the shot I was supposed to receive. Even those became less effective as I built up more and more resistance to them. She had to keep increasing the dosage. The pain, the boredom, the sleepless nights, and the constant trips back to the operating room all kept bearing down on me. The drugs were eating away at my will power. The things I might have done to pass the time I could not do. I liked to read but I could not hold a book or easily turn the pages with my heavily bandaged hand. I might have solved the problem, but I couldn't stay in any one position very long because my body ached if left in one position. If I had to move my body, I would also have to move the book and that was difficult to do.

The other thing I missed the most was a good night's sleep. I could sleep only sporadically because the pain kept the brain on edge. I always thought of the analogy of a set of electrical lines that had been knocked down in a storm and were whipping back and forth across the road, sparks flying as the current surged in irregular snaps of energy when the lines touched the ground or each other.

That's the way I pictured my mind and the pain signals it was getting from those raw nerve ends flopping around throwing off erratic signals.

And there was always the phantom pain in my stump. This pain was generated from nerve ends that had been severed in the arm. My brain still sent signals automatically to the hand and arm but the signals were shorting out in the flesh around the end of the stump. The signals sent back to the brain gave a false impression that hand and arm were still there and functioning. At night I would take a couple of "big reds"—sleeping pills—and if the one nurse was on duty, I'd talk her into giving me a "special" shot.

Unable to sleep, I would sometimes move about in the middle of the night, quietly speaking to the nurse as I passed by her station to sit in the semidarkness of the open ward.

In the ubiquitous soft light from the nurse's station long lines of blanket-covered men slept, their beds fading into a gray-black blur toward the end of the ward. The soft light made night gentle, smoothing out the sounds of groaning, crying, sleep talking, and other noises of troubled minds and restless bodies moving through the night.

Always during my secret scanning of the blanket-covered shapes I could pick out a pair of eyes watching me, another soldier silently tabulating the life of the night ward.

At 0300 or 0400 hours, the nurse at the night station prepared medicines or moved through the ward checking on the men. She would pull a blanket up around a man's shoulders, put her hand on someone's brow, answer a mumbled question, give a man a shot if he requested relief from the pain, and, like a friendly spirit of the night, add comfort and security by her presence.

What had me sleepless more than the pain was my fear of the pedicle graft. I knew what they were. I had seen them on other men.

The ward was a constant flow of wounded in various stages of the healing process. To an outsider some would have looked like monsters from science fiction created by a makeup artist to scare little children.

Used to replace flesh that had been burned or blown away, it was simply a tube of skin and underlying tissue cut from the patient's own body. Anyone who had a pedicle graft looked very freaky indeed. Imagine a strip of skin two or three inches wide and ten to twelve inches long somewhere on your body, for example, the stomach. The surgeon cuts this strip of skin and tissue entirely out except for one end of the strip which is left attached. The long strip is then rolled around once onto itself and sewed together lengthwise so the end product is a long tube of skin extending out like a frankfurter attached to the body. The detached end is then moved to the injured part of the body and reattached to the flesh. The end that has not been cut loose supplies blood to the tube keeping it alive until the reattached end has grown a network of blood vessels in the flesh where it has been surgically implanted. This regrowth takes about three weeks. At that time the end that had been keeping the tube alive is cut loose and leap-frogged to the injured area sustained now by the new blood vessels in the graft. Eventually, the fully attached pedicle tube of skin and flesh is cut to the shape of the wound and sewed into place. Skin grafts are then used to cover any raw wounds that remain.

Pedicle grafts are used to rebuild faces and to cover large areas of damage on limbs where muscles and tendons stand exposed. By themselves, skin grafts will adhere to the muscles and tendons and will severely limit their movement, whereas a pedicle graft is thick enough to allow the muscles and tendons to move more freely back and forth. Pedicle grafts are painful, however, and are not used if skin grafts suffice. Skin grafts are only the top layer of skin cells taken from one part of the body and spread out on an injured area. They leave a barely noticeable scar where they were removed. But a pedicle graft involves many layers of skin and tissue and therefore leaves a hell of a scar. The donor area of a pedicle graft is itself covered by skin grafts from another part of the body. The whole process is a real pain.

Skin and pedicle grafts come from a man's own body because the body will accept them easier. Due to an individual's particular genetic makeup, the body tends to reject grafts from others. Therefore, if a man can provide donor sites from his own body, the grafts have a very high chance of "taking."

A severe case of facial disfigurement sometimes had two or three of these tubal pedicle grafts swinging from his neck or face as he walked along the ward. As soon as one realized that the pedicle grafts were part of the healing process they became very easy to accept. The hospital was a good place to learn that physical ugliness and repulsion are not the mark of the man inside.

I had made friends with a Sergeant McAdov who had been in the hospital for two years while the surgeons had been rebuilding his face. An artillery man, McAdov had been destroying extra powder charges in an area outside his fire base in enemy territory. There had been three of them on the detail when they came under attack. They had been running up the hill toward the perimeter of their fire base when a bullet entered the back of his head. When the bullet exited the front of his face, it had ripped away everything below his eyes. His two friends had dragged him to safety.

The rebuilding of the facial bones and skin had been a long, laborious ordeal of two years. He had many more years to go. As long as I was in the hospital, I never saw McAdov without pedicle grafts. But in a way he was lucky. He was a deeply religious man in his thirties who had a very supportive wife. One day as we talked he took out his military ID card to show me what he had looked like. He had been a rugged, handsome man. I compared the good-looking man in the picture with the face of the man standing next to my bed and thought of the strength of his spirit, the wife who had stood with him through it all, his church which he believed in, and his good-natured personality. There was nothing repulsive about this man.

Because my stomach was to be the donor area, the pedicle graft would be attached directly to my arm. One horizontal cut, ten inches long, was made directly under my right breast. A vertical cut, five inches long, was made from each end. The cuts were deep enough to include the skin and fatty tissues underneath down to the rib cage. This flap of skin was pulled down and new skin grafts were taken from my legs and placed over the large raw area on the rib cage to protect it.

Then the old skin grafts were removed from my forearm and the arm was then folded over close to my stomach where the top section of the flap was sewed along the length of my forearm. My arm was now essentially a part of my stomach. It would remain that way for three weeks while blood vessels grew across from the flap to the arm. If I had been helpless before, I was doubly so now. My only arm was strapped to me like a straightjacket.

When I fought my way out of my usual combat dreams and awoke in the postoperative room to perceive how I was bound to myself I felt like the most miserable son of a bitch in the world.

Three or four days later President Johnson was to give a speech on television. All of us watched the evening news religiously because of its intense coverage of the fighting in Vietnam. Each night the war was brought to us in living color and the controversy raging over its wisdom and morality was *the* key topic for news media and editorialists. So far, we were distant from that controversy, deep in the protective womb of the hospital.

Of course, we criticized the hell out of the reporting if it wasn't accurate, but so far as we were concerned the war was just the war. It had changed our lives, spent its impact. What else could happen to us?

Regardless of my pain I wanted to watch the president's speech, so I stretched out my foot to the television set at the foot of my bed and turned the set on with my toes.

The blue seal of the president of the United States was replaced by the haggard features of the president. He announced two things I remember—he would suspend the bombing and he would not run for another term as president.

I looked at the calendar to mark this momentous date: 31 March 1968.

Four days later, on 4 April, Martin Luther King was assassinated and riots broke out in the large cities. As I watched the war news from Vietnam and the fighting in our own streets, I wondered just what the hell was happening to our country.

Mail Call: The Death of Bob Hutchinson, the Loss of My Wife

A few days later, during the first week of April, a Red Cross lady came to read my mail to me. I was all doped up and could not think very well, but I wanted to hear my mail even so. There was a tall stack, and I told her to save the two best letters for last, the one from Bob's parents and the one from my wife.

The letter from Bob's parents was shattering. Their sadness flowed from the words used to tell of Bob's death in Vietnam. He had been awarded the Distinguished Service Cross posthumously, and his citation related Bob's last moments on earth:

Second Lieutenant Robert S. Hutchinson, Infantry, distinguished himself by extraordinary heroism on 16 February 1968 while serving with Company A, 2d Battalion (Mechanized), 22d Infantry, 25th Infantry Division in the Republic of Vietnam. On this date, elements of Company A were conducting a reconnaissance in force operation in the vicinity of Tay Ninh when Lieutenant Hutchinson's platoon came under attack by antitank rockets, rifle grenades, automatic weapons and small arms fire from a Viet Cong Battalion positioned in well-fortified bunkers. Without hesitation, he immediately began directing the fire of his men on the enemy and, after an armored personnel carrier had crashed through a brick wall in front of the enemy positions, he led his men through the opening in an assault against the insurgents.

When heavy casualties were sustained, Lieutenant Hutchinson withdrew his men to regroup, covering their movements with his own fire. As the Viet Cong began a counter assault, he remained in his exposed position and fired into the charging Viet Cong ranks. Even though an enemy rocket exploded near him, Lieutenant Hutchinson continued to hold his position until his men had cleared the area. After supervising evacuation of the wounded, he again reorganized his men for another assault on the Viet Cong positions. While closing on the enemy, he was mortally wounded by automatic weapons fire. His courageous actions and determination were responsible for the eventual defeat of the fanatical enemy force. Lieutenant Hutchinson's extraordinary heroism was in keeping with the highest traditions of the military service and reflects great credit upon himself, his unit and the United States Army.

There was more in the letter, something to the effect that they were donating the ten thousand dollars of government insurance money to a Christian school in his name. But the letter was written in shock and said many things that I don't remember through my own despair of the moment.

The Red Cross lady sat silently next to my bed, not knowing what to say. She looked from the letter to my face and back to the letter. Her head was bowed and she scooted around in her chair. She cleared her throat and tried to speak but couldn't. Finally she murmured softly, "I'm sorry for your friend's parents."

I lay rigid on my back, staring at the ceiling, thinking of Bob as I had last seen him at his home near Los Angeles on my way to Vietnam. He had told me about the girl he would marry when he returned from Vietnam. We had laughed over his foolishness all the way to Huntington Beach where he and a neighbor spent half a day trying to keep me on top of a surfboard. He had taken me, his friend the country boy, to Disneyland and to Sunset Strip, where I had met those famous crazy ladies of California. At his parents' house he showed me the three eucalyptus trees he had planted in the backyard and several of his watercolors. We had fixed his parents' soft-water dispenser but had poured too much salt into the thing, which his father gently admonished us for. We had spent three wonderful days and nights together, raising hell and enjoying life.

Now he was dead.

The stench of my wounds broke the reverie. The odor reminded me of rotting jungle vegetation, of the putrid enemy bodies we left lying around after an ambush. And for one intense moment I saw Bob at the instant of his death.

I twisted my head around to where I could see the trees outside my window and the earth I loved. "Godspeed to my friend," I said to the sky.

We truly believed we would never die.

I could hardly speak, but I asked the Red Cross lady to read the letter from Linda. I needed good news.

The Red Cross Lady read.

Linda started her letter explaining that my disability had nothing to do with it, but she wanted me to divorce her when I returned home from the hospital. She wanted to remarry her first husband, who had reentered her life. I could have everything—the car, the furniture, the house—but I could not have my little girl, Teri Jo.

For the first time in many weeks, I became the missile from outer space. I destroyed the hospital, the Red Cross lady, my homeland of Indiana and Illinois. No one escaped my wrath. After I had spent myself, despair, helplessness, and depression set in. My heart and mind felt like quitting.

Oh God, what can I do when I lose my friend and my daughter?

When the Red Cross lady asked if she could do anything for me, I shook my head no. She quietly put the mail into the nightstand drawer, tucked the sheet around my shoulders, and left the room.

Flashes of lightning flickered across my vision. It was an effect caused by my eyelids blinking rapidly. I couldn't wipe the erupting tears with my hand, so I rolled my head to one side and then to the other to wipe the tears away on the pillow.

I cried for a very long time.

And there was no one to comfort me.

April

April moved at a glacial pace. My legs, feet, and buttocks healed rapidly, which made me feel good enough to want to be going places, but the pedicle graft prolonged my helplessness.

Every day for three weeks I had to visit a room dominated by the two plastic surgeons who oversaw the pedicle graft. One was a big bull of a man, completely bald. He was Colonel Hemphill, an old army man who, when I asked him what he did between the wars, answered "I fix noses." The other one was a civilian doctor who worked at Fitzsimmons on a reciprocal agreement with his civilian hospital. He was in his late thirties and had gray flecks in his hair and a wonderful bedside manner.

Their philosophies about drugs and pain were markedly different. Colonel Hemphill was hard as nails, and would not give me a pain shot before he started scraping blisters from the skin grafts over my rib cage. As he deftly swished the scalpel back and forth with one hand, cutting swiftly through the swelling blood blisters, he used the other hand to sponge the blood running down my side and into the cavity formed by the pedicle flap connecting my arm to my stomach. While working on my prostrate body, he would encourage me to

endure the pain without drugs, because the drugs weren't
worth it in the long run. He remarked that in his long army
career he had seen drugs harm far too many people. He
would have the orderly give me a cloth to clench in my teeth
against the pain.

When the other doctor was in charge, he always gave me
a shot if the colonel was absent.

But after the first few days of this skin-scraping procedure, I was such a nervous wreck it didn't make much difference who was scraping my rib cage. The pain from the
scalpel, the squirming from my tense body, and the sight of
my bright red blood running onto the sheets all combined to
leave me exhausted.

After the daily session I would clutch the bloody bandages to my side and return to my room, where I would collapse into bed and call for a shot to dull the pain. In the belief
that the shot itself offered as much psychological relief as
the drug, and in an attempt to withdraw us from dependence
on drugs, the medical staff these days would give us a shot
of "pain killer" composed of nothing except a harmless saline solution. But I could always tell the difference.

As I lay in bed trying to figure if they had given me a drug
or saline solution, and cursing them for their trickery, the
smell from the raw flesh left exposed on the inside of the
pedicle graft always seemed more pungent. I attributed the
intensified odor to the fresh blood from the scraping mixing
with the fluids from the open wound of the graft.

I was truly exhausted now from months of operations and
pain. This had been going on since 11 January and here it
was the middle of April. The sound of birds chirping carried
through the open window and the busy noises reminded me
it was spring. The farmers would be going into the fields back
home.

I had to get out of the hospital. "Christ," I thought,
"there are friends of mine who had been in here for three

years. How in God's name did they keep their sanity? I would go stir crazy!''

I concluded that they did it as I did it. Each day at a time, and look forward to the good things, no matter how small in scope. Everything had become important. Such as Friday nights.

This was the big night for those of us stuck in the hospital who could not go out. The Coors company donated beer every Friday for the hospital to distribute to the patients. A friend or a nurse would bring a beer into the room, stick a straw into the bottle, and set it next to the bed. Sucking beer through a straw gave it a weird, airy flavor, but I always happily drank the two I was allowed.

About the middle of April, the surgeons operated again. This time they cut the flap loose from my stomach and wrapped it around my forearm. They trimmed it to fit and sewed the edges shut with a drainage tube sticking through near the elbow. My arm was free to move and, if the pedicle graft "took," my fingers could be made flexible again. I hoped.

Three days later, the arm became infected and the graft swelled up tight with pus. I thought I was going to die from the pain. I was running a high fever and became slightly delirious. The duty doctor and nurses worried over the arm, cutting through the graft to drain the pus out, resewing the wound, reinserting the drain, and cleansing my body.

Later in the evening, the young nurse who had been "snitching" drugs came on duty. The pain and fever had caused me to drift in and out of focus with my surroundings but I was still able to remain coherent.

When she came to the doorway I lifted my head to see who it was. The lights from the ward were reflected in her large, dark eyes as she stood on the threshold staring at me. Her expression made me wonder if a terrible tragedy had just occurred. She was holding a medicine tray.

She came into the room, closing the door behind her. She moved to the side of the bed and set the small half-moon-shaped stainless steel tray on the nightstand. She put a thermometer in my mouth and touched her fingers to my neck to take my pulse.

A feeling of wrongness was in the room.

I studied her closely and could tell she was distracted. Her whole demeanor was one of nervousness. She was a thin, short, dark-haired girl who had always seemed slightly uncomfortable around the men in the ward. I thought I had detected a weakness which made her too vulnerable to the harshness of a combat ward. Perhaps this was why she nipped at the drugs and sometimes gave me an extra dose.

She was not mature enough to handle her emotions or the responsibility of her job. But neither one of us could have articulated those reasons then. She was twenty-two and I was twenty-three. Our common bond was the hospital environment with the frantic haste of medical teams rebuilding war-torn bodies. The immediacy of the moment was all that mattered.

Sweat from my body fever had soaked the sheets. She used a damp rag to wipe the perspiration from my brow.

"They told me when I came on duty you were having a rough time again, Fred."

"Oh, yeah. I feel like hell. . . . Boy, that cold rag feels good."

"I have something even better for you tonight, Fred," she said as she turned and picked up a hypodermic needle. She held up a small vial of clear liquid, turned it upside down, stuck the needle through the rubber cap until the tip went through the liquid, and slowly drew the plunger back, pulling the fluid through the needle into the plastic tube.

With a sense of foreboding, I glanced warily at the medicine tray. I recognized three powerful drugs.

Like a bad stretch of jungle trail, the ambience of the

situation was electric with danger signals. I became gut afraid.

"Naw, I don't think I'd better do this shit anymore. I'm feeling wasted enough as it is and I've got to get out of this hospital sometime." I paused. "I heard the birds singing this morning."

She pulled down the sheet and was searching for an unused spot to insert the needle into my skin. She ignored what I was saying and instead started talking about how when she was a little girl she had always dreamed of becoming a nurse. She had gone to nursing school and had run out of money but the army had given her a chance to complete her education in return for so many years serving as a nurse in the army. They had lived up to their end of the bargain by paying for her education, making her a lieutenant, and assigning her to an exciting job. However, she could not live up to her end of the bargain. She wanted out. She had never dreamed nursing would be like this. Cleaning up shit and piss and infection-rotted flesh and working long hours and strange times and seeing all these men blinded, burned, with limbs missing, bodies mutilated and . . . and . . . finally discovering that she didn't like this work. But she had to finish her obligation to the army.

"I've heard the same thing from guys who enlisted in the army, but they made it and so can you," I replied. She was rambling on, still diligently searching my skin. I began to suspect she was drugged beyond reasoning.

"Hey, look! I don't really want that shot."

"Are you in pain?"

"Yes, but I can take it."

"Oh, this is not too bad, just a little extra dope. You probably won't even feel the difference."

"Well, okay, if it's only a little extra." My resolve melted easily away. But my uneasiness increased. I knew I shouldn't have given in so readily. That in itself showed how dependent I had become. I was disgusted with my weakness and scared of the consequences.

She inserted the needle in the front of my hip, which I knew was dangerous. She pushed the plunger smoothly and the liquid flowed into my vascular system. Within seconds I knew I was in trouble. This was one powerful shot.

"Christ! Did you make a mistake? Wow! This is potent. Something's not right." I frantically questioned her.

The room started spinning. Slowly at first, I raised up, trying to stabilize myself. Meanwhile, she pushed the bed out from the wall, gave herself some kind of medicine, and climbed fully clothed into bed beside me. I was under the sheets and she was on the outside. This was not sex but an evil possession beyond our control. She was crying with an intensity which at first reached through even to my feelings. But I was rapidly becoming deranged as the room not only spun but started tumbling. The vertigo frightened me with a horror of being flung from the bed and the earth.

The drug's potency had not peaked. I became detached from myself and ran ahead of my body. I looked back to see me and the nurse wrapped in a cocoon of sheets on a bed in my room. We were dwindling in size as the bed tumbled over its axis into a vortex of brilliant psychedelic colors which swirled clockwise down into a dead black infinity.

My fear of death forced an animal, guttural scream from deep within my soul.

I remember nothing else. Later, I pieced together what happened. No one talked directly to me about it. Jan Gish, who could handle herself very well in any situation, was brought running by someone who had heard my scream. She had opened the door to my well-lit room, had seen me in shock, the nurse beating her fists against the wall, and had immediately assessed what had happened. She had called the duty doctor and together they had performed whatever technique was needed to bring me back to safety.

I was fuzzy for a few days afterward, and did not quite understand what had happened, but constant attention by the medical staff phased me swiftly back into normalcy.

The dark-haired nurse was transferred to Germany.

This crazy episode somehow put me over the hump, eliminating drugs, which had become the last major obstacle toward final recovery. Time went faster. I no longer lived in plodding, wearisome days composed of 86,400 seconds. The pedicle graft took well. On some days whole hours passed with pain unnoticed while I learned to use my artificial arm and hook and worked in physical therapy developing flexibility in my hand.

Hank's wife, Molly, bought me a pair of trousers and a shirt and underwear so I could leave the hospital grounds if the opportunity arose. My duffel bag arrived from Vietnam and I went over to retrieve my shoes and to see if all of my belongings had returned safely.

When I opened the bag, the musty, muggy smell of Vietnam assailed my senses, evoking pungent memories. I jerked erect, startled at the flashback's strength to move me in space and time.

But I was strong and running hard now to catch up on lost time. I didn't have the least inkling of which direction I was going, but that didn't matter. I could live with the memories of Vietnam, because to deny their existence would be to deny myself. Besides, I was damn proud to be a soldier. I still didn't understand fully the implications of the six o'-clock news. I retrieved my shoes, closed the bag, and signed the release form for the supply sergeant. He said he would be glad to store the rest for me.

What Happened to Your Arm?

The hospital was exceptionally boring now that I was feeling pretty good and doing only physical therapy. I began to

long for the world outside of the gates, and when Hank and
Molly offered to take me with them to the supermarket I
readily accepted.

It would be a good time to test myself.

For the last few weeks, I had been practicing with my
new arm, breaking it in around the hospital. I still felt extremely conspicuous having this plastic and metal contraption hanging from my body. I would surely be conspicuous
in the world outside, an oddity, but what I profoundly wished
for was to inspire neither sympathy nor fear.

I resolved to handle each trial as it happened. If the opportunity presented itself to satisfy people's curiosity and to
help them feel comfortable, strangers or friends, I would
explain how the arm and hook worked.

So it came to be that one day I found myself standing in
the middle of a supermarket, wondering what can of soup
to buy, when I became aware of someone staring at me. I
turned to see a little girl of seven or so and a little boy about
six, probably her brother, standing very still behind her.
Their eyes were open wide, and their mouths formed an "o"
of curiosity.

The little girl spoke. "What happened to your arm?"

"Are you Captain Hook?" the little boy piped up in awe
as he peered around his sister.

Oh oh! I thought to myself. Kids! I hadn't even thought
about kids . . . Let's see, quick, what do I say? Don't want
to scare them. What will they understand?

"Hello, there," I smiled, trying to appear friendly. "No,
I'm not Captain Hook. This is just my new hand. I lost my
real arm in a land-mine explosion." I looked at them hopefully, wondering if they understood. "I'm a soldier. Do you
know what a soldier is?"

They both continued to stare at the hook.

"Do you know what an explosion is?"

"Nooo," the little girl shook her head.

"Uh, how about . . . you know what a firecracker is?"

"Yes."

"Where's your other arm?" asked the little boy.

"Let's see, how do I explain this?" I wondered out loud. "Well, I was a soldier and a big firecracker blew my arm off. The army gave me this new arm, do you understand?"

"Where is your real arm?" the boy asked again.

"It's in Vietnam. Do you know where that is?"

"Uh uh." He shook his head.

"Why did you leave your arm there?"

I couldn't think of an answer to that one. "'Cause it wasn't any good anymore," I answered lamely.

"Why wasn't it?"

I couldn't think of an answer for that one either.

"It was hurt real bad so the army gave me this arm to use instead," I answered in a burst of genius. "It works almost as good as my real one. Here, see how I can make the hook open?"

They both moved back a step as the hook opened and closed. "I guess it looks pretty scary, doesn't it?"

They nodded silently. I agreed. It did look scary.

"I won't let this hurt you. I control it real good. Watch me pick up a can of soup." I opened the hook and then closed it around a soup can, pulling it from the shelf and then replacing it. "Pretty good, huh?" Yes. It was good.

The children nodded, but they still weren't so sure. "How do you make it do that?" the girl asked.

"There is a harness that goes behind my back and under my good arms. When I spread my shoulder blades apart, the cable tightens and pulls the hook apart and then when I relax my shoulders, these rubber bands pull the hook together."

"Oh." She looked perplexed.

"Can I have an arm like that?" The little boy had moved closer.

"You don't want an arm like this as long as you have

your real arm. This arm is only for when something real bad happens to your regular arm.''

I looked at both of them and said softly, ''You are not afraid of me now just because I have a hook, are you?''

''Andrea! John!'' Both children turned toward the voice of a heavy-set woman standing at the end of the aisle. ''Leave him alone!''

She scurried toward us, not looking at me except in nervous side glances, as she took them both by the hand. ''He doesn't want children to pester him. We have to go now.''

''That's okay,'' I interjected. ''They weren't bothering me. I was just explaining. . . .''

''Oh, no, I apologize, they shouldn't have bothered you. That was wrong of them.'' She cut me off, hurrying away in short nervous strides, pulling the children by the hand as they ran to keep up.

I think the mother meant well and I felt great about the children. They had understood. If this was the worst, I could handle it.

At the end of the aisle, the children looked back at me. I waved at them with my hook and they smiled, waving with their free hands as their mother pulled them around the corner.

CHAPTER 6
Home to Indiana
May 1968

The Okay

Hand clinic again. It was late April and I had been going to hand clinic and stump clinic once a week since I had arrived at Fitzsimmons on 11 February.

Would this ever end? I was healing. Physically, I was over the hard part and my body was a lot healthier than my mind. In the long battle between mind and body where each had alternately given up hope, the body had won, and now I had to get my mind straight.

I walked to my assigned spot and stood in front of the twenty or so doctors and residents seated in the room. Once again I was the focus of their attention as my doctor explained what he was doing to help me and why this or that method seemed to be working. He was very proud of the pedicle graft and described his surgical method and my success in regaining use of my hand. He held my arm up and traced with his finger along the seam of a scar.

I would be standing here in my blue hospital pajamas until the damn hospital collapsed, I thought.

As my doctor finished his monologue, silence fell. No one questioned him. I turned my head to look into his face, a face full of concern, not for my body, but for what had been injured in my mind, the injury he could not heal.

There was a gentleness in his voice as he asked me if there was anything I would like.

The thought had been buried there all the time and suddenly I said it.

"I want to go home."

I was shocked that I had said it and stared numbly at him, watching as his face broke into a smile.

"Well, I think that's a good idea, Lieutenant. What do you think, Doctor?" He turned to Colonel Brown, the man in charge of the group.

Colonel Brown glanced through his clipboard of notes, reading my history since 11 January 1968. The numerous operations, my growing dependence on morphine, acetaminophen, and Darvon because of those operations—he looked up to study me.

"Yes, I think you're right, Doctor. What the Lieutenant needs is to get away from here and go home."

My God, they were letting me go home. Now I felt only fear. I did not want to leave my protected environment in the hospital. Here was everything I had grown accustomed to and people who understood me. The hospital was now my home; its patients and staff were my family. Indiana was only a place I had left as a whole man full of confidence in myself and my ability to handle any situation. I would be a stranger there now. Nothing was as I had left it. I was a walking patchwork quilt. My wife wanted a divorce. My children would ask me questions. My family and friends would pity me.

But, even so, home. Visions of the Indiana countryside drifted across my thoughts. That was where I wanted to go, deep down. If I was to heal my mind, I must go home.

"When can I go? What about my pain shots? How long can I be gone? How about the changing of my bandages?" The questions flooded out.

It was decided I could leave the first of May. They would issue me a prescription for Darvon and my family could help change my bandages.

I went back to my ward, moving faster, more excited with every step. My fear was gone. Anticipation was crowding to the forefront.

"Hey, Benny, I'm going home!" I yelled, sticking my head into his room.

He turned his head toward me. "Hey, Fred, that's great!" He stood up and held his hand out. I rushed into the room and put my hand on top of his. I was afraid he would hurt me if I shook hands, but I wanted him to know I appreciated his gesture.

Benny had been depressed by my news that Bob had been killed, but Benny also was learning to cope with his blindness and the hard work helped him to overcome Bob's death. Benny's joy was an aura of warmth whenever I entered his room. With his usual direct-mindedness he had set himself the task of learning to read braille and was making good progress.

He wished me good luck and we agreed to get together when I returned from leave. I was going to get thirty days' recuperation leave.

I had little time to get ready. A uniform had to be prepared with my new rank and medals, leave papers had to be processed, and arrangements for transportation had to be made.

The cheapest flight I could get was a Continental redeye at 3:00 A.M. to Chicago. Then I could catch a Lake Central puddle-jumper down to Terre Haute. I called my wife to tell her what time my flight would arrive in Terre Haute and she said she would be there to pick me up.

The days passed quickly and finally came the night of my departure. That evening the nurses bid me farewell and wished me luck. About 10:00 P.M. one of the orderlies came into my room to help me on with my new arm and hook and assist me in getting my uniform on. We discovered a problem. There was so much nerve damage to my right hand that I could not open and close my pants zipper. I didn't feel that

I could approach a stranger at O'Hare Airport and ask him to unzip my fly, so I asked the orderly to bring me a paperclip and a long length of string.

I could handle large items fairly well. Therefore, I had him tie the string to the paperclip and bend out one end of the clip a little bit so that I could slip it through the little hole in the handle of the zipper.

I put the string and clip in my pocket. Would it work? Pulling the whole mess out of my pocket, I concentrated on picking out the paperclip and slipping the bent end through my zipper handle. Then I dropped the string to the floor, bent over, and stepped on it. As I straightened up, the string pulled the paperclip, which in turn pulled my zipper down. Then by wrapping my hand around the string, I could lift my arm and pull the zipper up. It worked like a charm.

A taxi took me to Stapleton Airport about midnight. A porter carried my bag down to the gate and I sat down to await my flight. I was surrounded in the waiting area by soldiers just out of basic training, going home on leave. Their brief introduction to the military had taught them that officers were distant people who performed mysterious functions and only came around when something went wrong or something had to be said that was really important—such as if they fucked up the coming inspection they would go on K.P. duty. Officers were to be avoided.

Now one had plopped right in their midst. They looked at me as if they couldn't believe I would be riding on the same airplane with them. I smiled to let them know I wasn't going to put any of them on K.P. duty tonight.

What must I look like to them? Only slightly older than they, I wore a uniform with more medals hanging from it than any one as young as I had a right to have. And a hook protruded out of my left sleeve. Part of my hand was bandaged and my uniform bulged where the other bandages patched my body. And I felt old.

I watched their kidding around with each other. How young they seemed. Were men this young really in my platoon in Vietnam? Surely not. They were still teenagers.

How many would still be alive or unmaimed a year from now?

As I boarded the Continental jet, a stewardess guided me to a first-class seat. I told her that was a mistake, that my ticket was for an economy seat. She smiled, fastening my seat belt; I was getting a first-class seat on this flight and no argument about it.

As the plane lifted from the runway I thought back to the last time I had flown on a Continental jet. I had been packed with one hundred sixty-eight other men flying from San Francisco to Vietnam. Another lifetime ago, I had been eager to go to war. Now I was going back home on a Continental jet, and the glory of war had faded with pain and a huge sense of loss and confusion.

Being one of the walking wounded did have its moments, however. The stewardess wined and dined me all the way to Chicago, treating me like a true V.I.P. That flight is the reason I travel Continental even today whenever I can.

The sun was breaking over the horizon as we landed in Chicago. The city had never looked so beautiful to me.

I had to fly standby on a small two-engine commuter aircraft to Terre Haute and again the stewardesses did their best to make me comfortable. I must have looked worse than I imagined to get all this attention. At one stop, I believe it was Bloomington, there was a danger of getting bumped off but one of the stewardesses talked to someone and I was allowed to remain on the aircraft.

Finally we landed at Terre Haute, Indiana. I exited the aircraft in the May sunshine, back home for the first time in nine months. I eagerly scanned the waiting people for my wife and two girls but they were not to be seen. I thought they must be in the small terminal but after frantically searching everywhere the sickening realization hit—no one was waiting for me.

The terminal soon emptied and I was left standing by myself.

I looked around at the empty terminal, the departing plane, and the wide lovely countryside around the airport. My fantasy of being welcomed home crumbled into dust.

I called home. No answer.

Standing at the window, staring at the state I loved, I wondered why I always seemed to fall into situations where I was not in control.

I paced the waiting room for an hour and a half, thinking deeply and effectively, for perhaps the first time, of my life and where I was going. In the hospital the thinking had not resolved anything, but during that ninety minutes everything started to fall into place for me. Whatever it took to get ahead in life I was going to do. The last nine months of my life had taught me that not God, or people, or the earth itself would take much notice of you. The only mark that I could leave on life would be of my own making.

I would not change overnight, but I knew that I would change to become more than I was.

The question in my mind was: What will it cost me?

When Linda pulled up in front of the terminal in our 1965 brown Mustang convertible I felt relief that she was only late and had at least arrived.

She had an excuse, but I have forgotten it. I sat in the passenger seat on the way from Terre Haute to Paris, Illinois, with my guts churning. I looked over at her. "You still want me to divorce you like you said in the letter? I know we talked on the phone about it, but I wanted to ask one more time if that's really what you want."

Linda took a drag from her cigarette while confidently steering with one hand over the concrete slab highway. "Yes, Fred, that's what I want. I have decided to remarry my first husband. I still love him. I should never have divorced him. Besides, you'll be okay. Some woman will be happy to marry you. You've got to understand I need someone who's going to be around and . . . well, you're never around and I don't think you'll ever be."

Gloomily I watched the highway ahead. I wearily settled back in the seat.

Soon the woman sitting next to me, chatting nervously away, would cease to be my wife. The two little girls, my stepdaughter and my daughter, would be taken from me to grow up not really knowing who I was. Our house in Paris would no longer be our home.

The First Night

Linda pulled into the driveway of our house and shut the motor off. I got out and stood in the grass near the small trees I had planted before leaving for Vietnam.

I had bought this house because it had a big yard. A small wood across the road lent a country atmosphere to the place.

I had lived there only a few weeks before shipping out for Vietnam, but that had been enough time to work in the yard. The house was just a small house, and never mine, but the labor of working in dirt was mine, the yard was mine.

August had been a bad month for transplanting trees but I had dug ten out of the ground across the road. I wanted to plant those trees before I went to war.

I couldn't afford to buy anything from a nursery, so I bagged the roots of the trees and dragged them across the road to holes I dug along the perimeter of my yard. It was those trees I was looking at now. Some had died, but a few had taken root. The dead ones would have to be removed, but not by me.

Sweeping my gaze over the yard once more, I went into the house, burning with hatred.

My daughter, Teri Jo, nearly two now, was babbling happily on her blanket when I came through the door. She had been born in October while I was in Infantry OCS at Fort Benning, Georgia, but the commander hadn't let me go home, so I didn't see her until Christmas when the army gave us leave. After that I didn't see Teri Jo much until Linda moved to be with me at Fort Gordon, Georgia, where we only lived a few months until my orders came.

The sight of my smiling daughter brought me up short. Christ! I had to accept my own stupidity, admit facts that I kept pushing away. I was a stranger here.

The aura of love that held Linda and her daughters was not extending its radiance to me. A pang of melancholy shot through me. I had not been home enough to nurture them with my love. Now it was too late.

I saw into the future as I studied Teri's face. It was a future without her. Oh God; it wasn't fair. The army had always had control of my time. But the fact was that *I hadn't been home enough*—to my daughter I was a stranger. I was stunned by the truth of this.

I stood and stared at Linda. Looking back on it, I count that moment as the end.

That night was a bad experience for both of us. Hatred, lust, and self-pity mixed equally in me as I lay staring at the dark bedroom ceiling. Linda was good to me. She tried to ease my wounds, both psychic and physical. But I was beyond reach.

I was thankful for the morning. Pain from my wounds had made me restless all night. After we got up, she helped change my dressings with the gentleness of a mother toward a child.

Then I was ready to leave. I wanted to run from this failure. I could not fight Linda; she was too strong and, besides, the battle was unwinnable. They always are between two people who once shared love and lost it.

My movements were desultory as I walked through the house, taking the few personal items stored in the back room in cardboard boxes. My clumsy attempts to pick up and carry the boxes using my strong nearly perfect hook and my very weak, imperfect hand embarrassed me. Linda wanted to help, but I refused her. I wanted to retain some sense of dignity, to display some strength. Rage at myself for being unable to control my physical disabilities forced tears into my eyes. I dropped a box while trying to open the car door.

As I bent down to retrieve it from the driveway, I kept my face turned away from Linda, standing by on the porch, still ready to help. The chore finished, finally, I looked at her.

"Well, I'm leaving," I said nonchalantly, afraid the tears would come again.

"Aren't you going to see Teri before you go?"

Emotions flew across my soul at that question. But my wall held. This woman, my child, our time together would go behind the wall. The briefest second delayed my answer, as I prepared to tell her no.

"No matter what you think of me, Fred, Teri is your daughter. You can never deny it. You are her father and it would be wrong to punish her because of what you think of me. When she gets older she'll want to know about you. I'll never say bad things or downgrade you in front of her, I can promise that. You have an obligation to Teri as her father and I will not let you hurt her by denying her existence!"

Surprised by the intensity of her love for Teri and confused by her demand of me also to love my daughter, I studied Linda's face. She was determined, ready to do battle to keep a father for Teri Jo.

The car door was open. I glanced at the interior, then at the house, knowing what was in my heart but unwilling to admit it, for if I did, my defense mechanism would prove vulnerable. I didn't need anybody. I was tough enough to survive anything. Even the loss of my daughter.

I laughed at my conceit and quailed at the fear sweeping through me. Was I so successful at survival that I was losing my humanity?

I turned my eyes to the north. Clouds were forming along another front that would bring rain in a few hours.

I turned the other way, looking over the roof of the Mustang to study one of the trees I had planted. A terrible truth was dawning in me. The small maple tree provided a focus while I groped to understand that truth.

Death and pain: in war, hospital, and home; from enemies, friends, strangers, and family. My protection and strength against all lay in solitude. I had been detaching myself from these things because solitude gave me power. Total solitude would give me total power. I was now a very lonely man. I felt, however, a need for the power of solitude. Recognizing the source of that power would now keep me from succumbing completely to it. Or at least I hoped.

"Yeah, you're right, Linda. I'd better see Teri before I go." I pushed by her into the living room where Teri lay on a blanket.

Much against my will, tears and sobs crushed the breath from me as I said goodbye, then walked fast to the car and drove away down the road.

It was over. I was alone.

I got a lawyer quickly, one of the advantages of a small town, and filed for divorce. It was granted in record time— ten days.

I drank for most of the rest of the day and met up with friends in town who asked me to go out with them in the evening. At the appointed time we arrived at a bar twelve miles from Paris. When we walked in, a live band was playing loud hillbilly rock and roll. After drinking all day, I was feeling no pain and spoiling for a fight. That was ridiculous, of course, in my condition. Dancing and talking with my friends did nothing to dispel my depression. My moodiness took the fun out of the evening for the rest of the group, who slowly withdrew, leaving me by myself. It was fine with me. Who needed them, anyway?

At midnight, toward the end of a set, my mind clicked into a phase I recognized as dangerous. It had happened before; a force swept me into an ecstasy of recklessness. Gleefully I wondered what I was in store for tonight. I was ready for anything to happen. I said goodbye to the group and went out to the parking lot. I wanted to drive.

I pushed the Mustang hard down the narrow asphalt country road at one o'clock in the morning. Holding the wheel steady with the hook, I leaned over with my hand to tune the radio on WLS out of Chicago. The savage beat of a rock band matched my mood as I turned my concentration back to the uneven dark road. The raised bumps where culverts crossed acted as ramps, lifting the Mustang up in barely controlled flight before it came slamming down onto the worn shocks and springs.

As the car slipped back and forth over the edge of control, I pushed harder, staying over the edge longer. I felt confident I could defeat it. I was invulnerable.

Before I realized it was upon me, I had torn through the stop sign at the intersection of Route 1. I slammed on the brakes, sliding in a gentle turn—slowly, it seemed—until the car side-slipped into a ditch, facing back the way I had come.

I got out to survey the damage. There wasn't any, so I retrieved a six-pack from the trunk, threw it onto the seat next to me, and gunned the car out of the ditch. Steering with the hook, I drove into town, beer in hand and listening to the radio, while deciding what I should do next. There was nowhere to go at this time of the morning and I didn't feel sleepy, but I needed a place to stay for the night.

I decided to visit Linda and stay there. After all, it was my house too.

I didn't recognize the car in the driveway as I pulled the Mustang up behind it and turned off the motor. Maybe it was her sister's or a friend's. But there were no lights on in the house to indicate visitors and nowhere for anyone besides family to sleep, except the floor.

With the speed of thought my mood changed from recklessness to despair. I stood on the porch knowing I should turn and leave, but I had to erase any doubt.

I knocked until the bedroom light came on and Linda came to the door in her robe. She stood with the door ajar.

"Is that you, Fred? What are you doing here?"

"I need a place to stay tonight."

"Well, you can't stay here."

"What do you mean I can't stay here? At least let me come in."

"No, you can't."

"I want to come inside." I looked behind her to see if anyone else was there.

"Fred, you're drunk. I don't think it's a good idea for you to hang around. You'll wake the kids. Fred, go away."

I left and drove down the road out into the country, where I stopped the car. After rummaging around in my stuff, I found the .38 Colt revolver I had won in a card game at Fort Gordon before the war. The shells were in a belt wrapped around the pistol.

Stepping out of the car I laid the weapon, bullets, and belt on the hood. I shook from the cold, the alcohol, and my rage as I tried to load the gun. The nerve damage to my hand made it hard. Finally I managed to use my hook and damaged hand to push bullets into the pistol.

Surprised at the weakness of my grasp, I was not sure if

I could hold and fire the gun at all, let alone be accurate with it. The familiarity of the weapon calmed my nerves. I walked across the road, over a ditch, and onto a plowed and disked field. "Must have done this field early," I thought, "before the rains came."

I held the gun in profile up close to my face, the barrel pointed straight up at the sky, the trigger mechanism in line with my eyes.

My thoughts swung: With this gun I can kill. Killing does not bother me. I have killed enough to know. Some soldiers in line of duty have had guilt because they killed. At first I worried when I had none. Then I worried that it was so easy to kill.

Yeah, easy. And look where it's got me, standing out here in a Goddamn cornfield going crazy. We were sent to Vietnam to kill and we did a good job, but I am in the "world" now. I can't let the killing in Vietnam pass over to the world with me. I've got to leave that behind or I'll kill myself. I had a chance to die, plenty of chances to give up, but I didn't.

I lowered the pistol until the barrel pointed into the dark. "Take that," I growled through clenched teeth. When I pulled the trigger the gun fired and jumped, recoiling. A bolt of excruciating pain surged from my hand up the length of my arm. The pistol fell into the dirt at my feet.

Having no left arm to cradle my hurt right hand with, hunched over groaning in pain, holding my arm against my side, I yelled obscenities at the dark.

After searching in the dark for thirty minutes, I finally found the gun and trudged with it back across the field, ditch, and road, where I tossed everything into the back seat and drank the last of the beer. Then I pulled into a lane leading back to a wood I remembered and slept fitfully in the car until morning.

I was still not home.

"Mom"

I awoke in the gray dawn. A misty rain was falling through fog.

"Well, great welcome home, Fred," I laughed to myself as I thought of the past thirty-six hours. My body ached like hell and my artificial arm had been a damn nuisance whenever I shifted in my sleep, but I was getting used to it.

I drove to a truck stop outside of town and sat at the end of the counter drinking coffee while I got my thoughts in order.

What did I expect back here? I had wanted to go home. I had had a strong urge to get back among familiar things.

Now that I was here, I felt uneasy, unfulfilled. There was something missing but I couldn't pin it down. It was exhilarating to be free and to be on home ground, but I sensed I was a stranger.

I deeply yearned to know exactly what had happened within me over the past nine months. The rigors of combat, the horrific effects of pain, the loss of an arm: It was important for me to come to grips with these, to analyze their effects on me.

After going through all I had endured, some good had to come out of it. Otherwise, what would be the sense of all my suffering?

I needed a reason for all those things.

I would spend this month searching back through my life, exploring the places that had meaning to me and visiting the people I knew.

This was May, my birthday month. My favorite time of year. I would be twenty-four on the 27th. I would have the answer by then.

Satisfied with this plan, I studied my reflection in the mirror behind the counter. I was supposed to visit Mom this afternoon. I had better shave and get cleaned up, which I did at an old friend's house, and soon after was heading east out of Paris to Terre Haute.

While driving, I experimented with the hook. How easy it was to handle the car using it and the arm together. The Ford had an automatic transmission, but I bet I could handle a standard shift.

A rain squall swept across the car. The raindrops pattered the hood and just as quickly dried and disappeared. I rolled the window down and drew in a deep breath of wet spring air.

Jesus H. Christ, it was good to be back.

I reached in my coat pocket and pulled out two bottles of Darvon. They were the only pain killers I had left the hospital with. One bottle was my prescription and the other was a bootleg bottle I had acquired from the "network." I hadn't taken any since I had left the plane.

"Fuck you!" I grunted and heaved them both out of the open window. I watched in the mirror as they tumbled into the grassy ditch.

"That shit almost killed you, Fred." With a sense of relief I fixed my attention on the narrow cement road. I would be at Mom's house in another forty minutes.

The wheel of life keeps turning, I ruefully thought as I parked in front of Mom's house. I have come back to the place I wanted so much to leave. Couldn't wait to get out of high school so I would be on my own. Impossible—a person can leave everything behind but can never escape the blood that brought him into the world.

I slammed the car door and paused beside the brown convertible while I took my bearings. Mom and Dad had moved to Terre Haute after my high school graduation in Marshall, Illinois. I had never lived in this one-story white stucco house on the corner of 23rd Street between Wabash and Ohio avenues.

I walked to the back door. Rarely did anyone in my family use the front door of any house we lived in.

Now I was excited at the prospect of reunion. Not only was I a returning war hero, I was a man and would be treated like one.

Suddenly, my family burst out of the back door to greet me, and simultaneously I glimpsed the blur of a small tomcat-sized white and black mongrel rushing out of a doghouse under the tree next to the walk.

My shouts of joy at seeing my family were overtaken in my throat and a bellow of surprise, pain, and rage surged out. "Yeehoallh," I screamed as the mongrel latched onto my right calf, his sharp teeth piercing the new scar tissue.

"Son of a bitch! Get this motherfucking dog off me," I shouted, dancing in a circle shaking my leg furiously, trying to dislodge the dog who was not about to relinquish his mouthful of leg.

Mom stopped to gain a better command voice.

"Spot! Let go boy, let go, that's Freddie!"

"Damn dog don't know it's me, Mom," I hollered at her, "but he'll know it soon enough when I hit him with this hook." I swung my hook down at the dog, murder in my intent. But the movement of my shoulder unlocked the elbow, causing the forearm to swing sharply, bringing the hook's point, with all the force of my swing, into my knee-cap.

The pain numbed all other pain and then all pain was swamped by rage.

"Yahaaa, you motherfucker, I'm going to kill you!"

A cloud of dust had risen up around us as my brother Rex scooted around trying to grasp Spot and dodge my swings and kicks. My brother Wayne and my sister Pam stood close by, yelling encouragement. Mom kept admonishing Spot to let go, me not to hurt Spot because he was just protecting the house and doing his job, Rex to get Spot off me, and Wayne to stop laughing.

Wayne was slapping his knee and laughing while encouraging Spot not to let go.

"Get him, Spot, sic him," Wayne coached gleefully.

Pam kept saying, "Oh, Freddie, Spot doesn't mean it."

"Fred, dammit, hold still long enough till I can grab Spot," Rex told me above the growling, laughing, cursing commotion.

Somewhere during all this Spot let go and like all smart small dogs tried to run out of range. But as he went by I swung my foot and caught old Spot right in the rib cage with the toe of my shoe.

Spot responded with a satisfying yelp, but like a Bantam rooster he turned on me, barking and snarling like he was going to come at me again.

"Keep that son of a bitch away from me or I'll kill him. He bit right into my leg wound," I exclaimed while examining my pant leg and skin where Spot's teeth had gone through.

"Don't worry, Freddie." Pam hugged me. "Spot has had his rabies shots."

"Are you sure about that? Cause you know how Mom is about putting off things," I replied as Mom and I hugged each other.

Mom's smiling face was wet with tears, which surprised me because I didn't remember her crying before. She pushed me back and held me at arm's length, looking me over.

"Hey, Mom, I'm sorry I kicked your dog. He just surprised me and in combat I learned to react fast to surprises." Damn, I felt bad about kicking Mom's dog. She loved her dogs and cats and was always hurt whenever they came to grief.

With a sudden swelling of my chest, the breath caught in my throat and I saw Mom for the first time in my life, not as my mother, but as a forty-one-year-old woman who furiously loved her six children and wanted them to have a better life than she had had.

And what did she think of me? Here was her first born son returning from a war with an amputated arm and other wounds and with no good prospect for a future.

I clasped Mom to my chest and stroked her hair while my eyes blurred with moisture as I told her, knowing for the first time in my life what it meant, "I love you, Mom. It is good to be home."

Close behind that emotion was a determination to protect her from further hurt by convincing her not to worry about her dreams for me. This was the first time she had seen me since last August so my gauntness and, worse, my hook had to be a shock. I felt a need to put her at ease.

I parted from her and swung my hook up just as if it were a hand. "See what the army gave me. This hook works almost as good as a hand. Look at this." I opened the hook, put the spread steel pincers around her hand and gently relaxed the pressure on the cable, allowing the hook to close softly on her fingers.

My brothers and sister were clustered around us, watching intently as I opened the hook, releasing her hand.

"See, it works real good. I can do everything with it." I went on putting my artificial arm through its paces, showing off the versatility of movement available to me through plastic, steel, and nylon.

Mom's relief was easy to see in her face as she immediately accepted my confident assessment of the artificial arm. The rest of the family, true to Mom's upbringing, quickly accepted me as I presented myself. My reward for putting them at ease was the normalcy we felt as we walked toward the house.

Wayne wanted to borrow the keys to my Mustang. Rex

was bringing some of his friends over to meet me. Pam was going out with a friend.

They all promised to be back in time for supper. In my honor. Mom had come home early from work to cook. Fried chicken, mashed potatoes and gravy, green beans, tossed salad, iced tea and milk, and sliced white bread. I knew the menu before I went into the house. It was Mom's special meal for guests.

Although I had never lived in this house, the atmosphere was home. Mom liked to have things happening and, as we visited while she cooked, the flow of sounds and people provided a backdrop of activity I had grown up thinking was normal for any family. Two television sets tuned to different stations were playing in different rooms. A radio blared rock music. Rex and Wayne's rowdy friends rumbled in and out of the house like miniature thunderstorms. I was introduced to their girl friends as war hero brother.

The noise was overwhelming. I was especially sensitive to noise after being in the hospital for four months. To ease my nerves, I went through the house turning off the television sets and radio, but shortly afterward, whoever was passing by reflexively turned them back on. I was astonished at my family's need for noise.

At supper the noise and traffic barely paused. My brothers' friends stopped in for a meal and made themselves at home, insensitive to Mom's feelings of special occasion. Perhaps only I noticed the rudeness. Probably I had been as insensitive before the war.

After supper the kids left Mom and me alone. I was eager to talk to her about life, the deep stirrings in me that the war had caused, my feelings about death, the pain of my wounds, and my growth into manhood, but most of all that I had thought so much about Mom, as a woman who struggled to give her children love, independence, dreams, and a positive outlook on life. I wanted to give something back.

Somewhere along the line in the hospital, I began to know why I was surviving so well. It was Mom's influence on me. And just as powerful in its own way was Dad's. He reacted to trouble by striking out physically. These were invaluable to survival and I would learn to understand their effect on me later.

Now was a time for what Mom had taught me—the beauty of life and the world around me and the positive side of everything as well as a buoyant enthusiasm and boundless curiosity.

Yes, I did have a lot to thank them for, but as I sat at the kitchen table smoking cigarettes and drinking a beer with Mom, I was embarrassed to say these things.

I was her son and I had been to war, the most manly of all endeavors, but I sensed she felt closer to me than she ever had before.

Perhaps it was the telegram.

"Mom, let me see the telegram they sent when I got hit. I want to read it."

"Sure, I've got it here someplace." she said, riffling through a stack of envelopes on the mantel. "Here it is."

I pulled the two sheets out of the Western Union envelope and hunched forward on my elbows on the kitchen table while Mom lit cigarettes for both of us and handed me one.

Mr. & Mrs. Frederick Downs, Sr., Don't Phone The Secretary of the Army has asked me to express his deep regret that your son, Lieutenant Frederick Downs, Jr., was placed on the seriously ill list in Vietnam on 11 January 1968 as the result of multiple metal fragment wounds to the body, with traumatic amputation of the left arm above the elbow and neuro vascular damage to his right arm. He was on a combat operation when hit by fragments from a hostile booby trap. In the judgment of the attending physician his condition is of such severity that there is cause for concern, but no im-

*minent danger to life. Please be assured that the best med-
ical facilities and doctors have been made available and
every measure is being taken to aid him. You will be kept
informed of any significant changes in his condition. He is
hospitalized in Vietnam at the 2nd Surgical Hospital, APO
San Francisco 96394. Address mail to him at that address.*

*Kenneth G. Wickham, Major General USA, The Adjutant
General (46).*

I looked up at Mom. "Jesus, what a telegram. What did
you think when it came? How was it delivered?"

"Well . . ." Mom paused to light a cigarette and after
inhaling the smoke picked up her coffee cup and stared into
it. She exhaled the smoke, sipped the hot coffee, and, setting
the cup down, began to talk about that other time.

"He was just a delivery man from Western Union. When
I went to the front door and saw who he was and what he
was carrying, I knew it was bad news. Telegrams are always
bad news. As soon as I signed for it, he turned and quickly
walked away. I guess he had delivered enough of those telegrams that he didn't want to wait around to see my expression. I figure I looked pretty bad just worrying about what
was in it."

She took another sip of coffee and returned to her story.

"You can't imagine what that telegram did to me. I don't
cry much. I keep everything like that down deep inside because you have to be tough to survive this life. I don't cry,
but I feel.

"You were my first baby. Everything that happened to
you as you were growing up was always a first for me. The
first day you went to school I took you down to the gravel
road in front of the farmhouse on the Glasscock place and
helped you get on the school bus. I cried then. Hell, the other
five kids, I never batted an eye sending them off to school.

"Your first tooth falling out, your first date, your first
driver's license, being on the honor roll in grade school; all

of those little things were my first, because you were my first.

"After I read the telegram, I wanted to get on a plane to fly to Vietnam where you were in the hospital. I wanted to see you, but I didn't know how to find you even if you would be there when I arrived. Besides, we didn't have any money.

"I took the telegram into the kitchen to give to your Dad who was still pretty well paralyzed from his stroke. Of course, he started making plans to have Pam take him to wherever you were hospitalized, regardless of whether we had any money or not. I talked him out of that until you returned to the United States.

"I was in a combat zone myself around here, what with me in the process of divorcing your Dad; we were being evicted from the house, the hospital and medical bills from his stroke couldn't be paid, and your Dad's old business deals were collapsing everywhere, bringing people banging on the door in the middle of the night wanting money.

"And then receiving this telegram. They always bring bad news.

"Somebody had to be tough, and I've always been tough. I was working two jobs just to keep us fed. I felt real bad I couldn't be with you, but I couldn't, so that was that.

"I've always regretted not flying to wherever you were after you got wounded, but I knew you would make it, Freddie." Mom reached out and put her hand over mine.

I looked into her face and understood the cruelty parents bear during a war. Also there was a change between us now. We both realized my childhood was gone. In a way we were strangers. What could we say except the familiar?

"How's your leg, Freddie?"

"It's okay."

"Don't worry about rabies. The last time I got Spot out of the pound they had given him a rabies shot and made me pay the bill before they let him go. That was only two months ago."

"Thanks, Mom. Not that I didn't trust you or anything like that, but you do tend to put things off."

"You want to stay the night? You can have Wayne's bed. He won't mind."

"Okay, Mom. That'll be nice."

"Do you still hurt anywhere, Freddie?"

"Naw, just a little ache here and there, Mom. Don't worry, I'm okay now."

"Did they treat you right in those army hospitals?"

"The best, Mom, the best. Hey! Let me help you do the dishes," I said as I stood up and started collecting the dirty dishes from the table. I was standing next to the sink when Mom came up behind me and put her arms around my waist.

"I love you, Freddie."

I looked at my gaunt reflection in the window above the sink. I was beginning to feel at home. "I love you too, Mom."

Grandma Downs's Farm

At noon the next day, dressed in my uniform, I kissed Mom goodbye and drove the Mustang at a furious rate up Route 63 to Clinton, Indiana, where I turned east and crossed the Wabash River, then north on Highway 41, heading toward Rockville. The closer I got to Grandma's the faster I wanted to go. As I approached Turkey Run State Park, about twenty miles from Grandma's, the speed burned out to be replaced by a warming of my spirit.

Everywhere were landmarks familiar to me since my childhood. I drove through the countryside I knew so well until at last I turned into the gravel road south of Grandma's.

The farm was as I remembered it. A small white house

stood nestled in a group of maples, walnuts, and locust trees on top of a gentle knoll. A weather-beaten gray wooden barn sat on a neighboring knoll to the south. A small stream meandered through a pasture between the knolls to pass under a small narrow cement bridge on the road ahead of me. The stream wound through a wood and passed from sight around another small hill.

My chest swelled from sudden emotions and tears filled my eyes at the realization that I had nearly missed coming home to the place and people I loved. I pulled my Ford off to the side of the road near the stream I had crossed so many times. Grandpa and I had walked down this gravel road to do the chores over at the barn. Partially healed wounds sent waves of pain through my body as opening the car door proved to be almost more than I was capable of.

I crossed the roadside ditch and stiffly climbed a short distance to sit down next to a maple where I had carved my initials a lifetime ago.

Bracing myself with my hook, I shifted my aching body to a more comfortable position so I could study the house over on the hill. Only Grandma lived there now. Grandpa had died ten years before.

All of this is what I am. It would have died with me on that bloody cot at Chu Lai.

But my heart had quit beating! I had died!

My hand pressed into the grass; my fingertips dug into the earth reassuringly.

Indiana was my home. I was Home!

This was real. Springtime in Indiana, the month of May. The earth reflected my mood of a new awareness of life. Everything around me was gloriously alive in the heady experience of emerging from the dormant period of winter.

I thought of my men in Vietnam. Each had memories special to him and to those around him. Like me, their lives with family and friends had not been recorded for history, but those interactions were the wellsprings of American consciousness. The dead had taken their memories with them, the loss barely noticed, except by those who had shared those memories.

To those who had shared, the loss was an emptying of their souls and would never be forgotten. The memories: the intimate moments between grandpa and grandson, the third grade class picture, seventh grade puppy love, the special gift one Christmas, his dog, his room containing his belongings, the car he left behind for his brother to take care of, the sister who teased him.

All of these exquisite moments of humanity were gone.

A robin landed next to me, breaking my reverie. I looked over to the house on the hill.

Grandma came out of her house and stood in the yard under one of the tall maple trees. Her pink dress was blowing in the breeze as she gazed apprehensively in my direction, wondering if it was me over here on the hill next to the stream.

I slowly pushed myself up, bracing myself against the tree until I could stand as tall in my uniform as my bandages would allow. My eyes were full of tears as I waved to my Grandma across on the hill and she waved back.

I left the car where it was. I preferred to walk up the gravel road so that I could relive the memories of every footstep that I had taken before with Grandpa.

I was home.

Nothing in the world feels so good as returning to a place and to the people whom you love.

Grandma was walking down the yard as I limped toward her.

The first experience a wounded soldier has when coming home is the pure joy and delight of those who love him, expressing their happiness that he is alive.

Memories to hold a lifetime: the hugs, the crying, laughing, the nervousness of asking about the wounds, thanking God you're alive, the moment of holding someone special as floods of feelings and tears bind you together.

Reaching one another, we hugged as sobs wracked my body from happiness and relief. Grandma told me with tears in her eyes that I was alive through the grace of God. He had not meant for me to go yet because he had something planned for me.

I didn't argue. I only knew for sure that I was truly home.

The Field

The visit the day before with Grandma had been beyond my expectations. As I listened to the stories she told about her grandma, it occurred to me how important family continuity was to the individual. I was also finding answers to questions I had thought about in the hospital.

Closing the gates behind me, I had driven to the middle of the farm when the rain started. I had now stopped. Low clouds scudded rapidly to the northwest, carrying the end of the rainshower away. The windows of the Mustang were starting to fog up, blocking my view of the plowed field and the woods bordering it on the south side. I had stopped when the rain started to fall. The grassy lane cutting across the middle of Grandma's farm was only used by farm machinery. The absence of any traffic made the lane a lonely but comfortable place for me to think.

I opened the car door and, with an effort to avoid hurting my wounds, stepped out of it to stand in the grassy lane. I walked for a hundred meters or so, arriving at an enormous elm that had stood solitary for seventy years or more at a turn in the lane.

The sun broke through a rift in the clouds, lighting the green so dramatically that the impact to my eyes was the same as a ringing of small bells might be to my ears. The smell of wet dirt and of growing and decaying things saturated my nose. I sucked the smell deep into my lungs.

With a moan of pleasure at being alive to appreciate this day, I slowly went down on my knees, leaning forward to press my hand into the damp grass. My hook sank into the earth. I lowered myself onto the earth until my body was fully stretched out.

My fingers swept the raindrops from a patch of grass a few inches in front of my nose. Resting my chin in my fist and moving my artificial arm around until it was comfortable, I devoted all of my attention to that patch.

There was so much to earth I had not noticed. Different kinds and sizes of grass, weeds, bugs, dead twigs, leaves, and other organic material. Diversity.

"Why, this is fascinating!" I murmured out loud. All of these had been under my nose my whole life. Up to now I had been looking at a mosaic of the earth—the fields, the woods, the pastures—taking them for granted because they had always been there, and not wondering or caring that they were made up of smaller pieces.

I had made a discovery—not about the earth, but about myself.

On 11 January, only five months ago, the day I had stepped on the mine, I had lain on the trail waiting for the dust-off, not really believing it made any difference if the chopper made it or not, because I knew I was dying. My stubborn nature would not allow me to admit defeat, but I knew rationally that defeat was possible. Part of my last thoughts were of the farm—this farm where I now lay.

I rolled onto my back to lie on the path the way I had lain on the trail when I was dying. A feeling of déjà vu overtook me as low clouds moved across the sky. The sky into which I was staring turned gray, Vietnam gray. The feeling of having returned to that day was so strong that I lifted my head to reassure myself where I was.

Why would I deliberately simulate the 11th of January? Why roll over on my back? Was this notion the representation of a deeper urge, a death wish? "Death wish," I muttered. There, I had said it aloud. Did I have a death wish? It could be true—my actions in Vietnam and after might even support the idea. Charging into action every chance I got; refusing to leave the field after my second, third, and fourth wounds; deliberately anxious to become involved in firefights; and the other night—driving like crazy. What did all of that mean if it didn't mean that I had a death wish?

I stared at the gray sky, impervious to the wetness soaking through my clothes. Slowly I raised my hook, outlining it against the sky.

I thought of a short story I had read about a man in the Civil War who was going to be hanged from a bridge. His mind had been full of the thoughts of home and family and how desperately he wanted to see them before he died. He wanted a second chance at life because, just as he was on the verge of dying, he was realizing how much life had to offer. He was pushed from the bridge but the rope broke, dropping him into the river. During his escape and return home, he observed the leaves and other things around him with a clarity he had never seen before. Just as he reached home, the man and the reader realize that these are the thoughts of a man in seconds before his death. Because the rope did not break and the man's last thoughts are a fantasy of a second chance.

A small mist of rain blew across the field leaving fine rain droplets covering my body. I had been given my second chance. I smiled as I intently observed the hundreds of raindrops clinging to my clothes and felt the moisture against my skin.

This was no dream. This was life. I was appreciating it for the first time because I finally knew what death was, and by knowing that I knew what life was. In youth and war I had believed I was immortal.

I had no death wish. On the contrary, I had been looking for the meaning of life and had finally found it here in this field in Indiana.

Settling Back In

My cousin Jack and his wife, Jeri Lee, lived on a farm about two miles from Grandma Downs. After visiting Grandma, I drove over to their place. The small one-story farmhouse with three outbuildings stood at the corner of a gravel road. Farm machinery was parked haphazardly around the buildings. A few old majestic maples stood grandly by the house.

When I pulled up in the yard, all the emotions of coming home once again flooded through me. Jack and I had been like brothers growing up. Our fathers' farms had not been far apart. I had been best man at his wedding and he at mine.

He, Jeri Lee, and I shared a multitude of memories. After a warm reception, they offered me a couch to sleep on, to which I readily agreed. I ended up staying the whole month. Their home provided a convenient base of operations from which I ventured forth on my quests and returned at any hour of the day or night.

This turned out to be important because I was under no pressure from them of any kind. They offered me almost total freedom while I searched for something within myself.

Losing my arm had been a traumatic experience both physically and mentally. Combat had raped rationality. Many of my men and close friends had been killed or wounded.

I *had* to find a meaning in all of this. It was impossible for me not to try.

The evening news confused me. Venomous attacks by anti-war groups against the war and even against all who wore the uniform stirred emotions of anger, frustration, and bewilderment. The increasing doubt about America's role in Vietnam being expressed in editorials, by politicians, and by other influential people was discouraging.

I began to dodge an ominous feeling of alienation. No one seemed to know or care about the men who were doing the fighting. "To hell with who's right or wrong!" I thundered out one night at the television set. "What about the sacrifices being made by those guys over there?"

Some nights after watching the news I would feel utterly perplexed and depressed. I couldn't make up my mind whether my men and I had been cheated or not. For protection I discovered myself always referring to Vietnam in terms of my platoon. I didn't know anything about Vietnam except my personal experiences. That was the one rock I clung to. I developed an attitude of "Fuck them" whenever anyone started spouting off about Vietnam. I just wasn't in the mood to argue about Vietnam. I was done with it. I wanted to get on with life.

I was supremely confident I had done a damn good job of soldiering. No one could take that away from me. I was extremely proud of being a soldier. This was an absolute in my thinking.

Luckily, except for a few minor episodes with people, the only time in May that I defended myself concerning Vietnam was when I discoursed with the television set and the car radio. My private monologues were valuable in preparing me for the future when I returned to college, but at the time I was just blowing off steam. I had no idea of what was ahead of me when I returned to Denver.

I just concentrated on being home.

Time had crawled in the hospital but it grew legs and sprinted in May. I drank, I ate, I ran around, I went places for entertainment. I visited family and friends. I went a little crazy. I had fun.

Many wonderful things happened to me and many fine people treated me specially. One woman was sublime. I can never repay my debt to her. My family helped me fit back in at home as naturally as could be. They took pride in me and shared my successes with their friends. Once I was riding with Uncle Marvin in his truck on the gravel road between his farm and Grandma's place when he saw a neighbor driving toward us. Uncle Marvin stopped in the road and got out to talk with his neighbor, who had also stopped. Uncle Marvin introduced me as his nephew who had gone to Vietnam and "lost his arm over there."

I was standing next to Uncle Marvin and as he described my pedicle graft he asked for my arm. I held it out. He unbuttoned the shirt sleeve and rolled the sleeve up so he could point out this "pedicle graft operation." The neighbor was impressed with both the graft and the artificial arm.

This innocent curiosity was expressed over and over by people who were intrigued and fascinated by the ingenuity used in piecing me back together again.

I discovered a keen gratification in sharing knowledge so other people could benefit. With my personality, this was a positive and natural course for me to follow. The interaction made me and others more comfortable about the artificial arm. The arm became an asset because of the remarkable impact it had on people, and actually enhanced my encounters with people.

It wasn't all smooth sailing. I was still self-conscious to a degree and would occasionally have to take a deep breath before I walked into a crowd of strangers. If I had trouble using my hand and/or hook to open, carry, or otherwise manipulate something, I would become flustered because I imagined people might see me and feel pity. But I learned to take a deep breath and work out a solution, even if it meant asking for help once in a while.

Sometimes I tried to act so nonchalant I became conspicuous by my behavior—like the time I took a girl over to Danville, Illinois, to a club where we could listen to a live band and dance. We were sitting at a small round table in the middle of the crowd when I decided to go to the bathroom. I wanted to be real cool about this so I excused myself and pushed back the chair to stand up. An action like this was always tough the first time because there was a little voice at the back of my mind nagging me that everyone was staring.

They weren't, of course. Except for a few naturally curious glances, people didn't pay much attention, but I was still a little nervous at this stage. I strolled around the crowded table, toward the rest room sign. The dance floor was full of couples gyrating to the rock band.

With a sigh of relief I pushed through the door of the rest room into the relative quiet. I fumbled with my zipper trying to grab hold of the little lever with my numb fingers. Because of the nerve damage I couldn't do detail work with my fingers unless I could see to guide my fingers.

I hoped no one would come in while I was fumbling around or they might think I was playing with myself. Finally I accomplished my mission, washed my hand, and pushed open the door. There were four or five girls standing outside the door giggling. The band had taken a break so everyone was at their seats. I got the uncomfortable feeling that some of the people were glancing out of the corners of their eyes at me and were smirking.

It wasn't my imagination, either. By God, they were looking at me funny.

I made myself walk calmly back to my table, but my hook felt like a cannonball sticking out of my sleeve. I hastily sat down and blustered to my date, "I guess these people never saw a hook before. I swear they were staring at me when I came out of the men's room."

She chuckled, "I don't think it was the hook, and you didn't come out of the men's room. That was the ladies' room!"

"Oh." I looked guiltily back toward the door. Two of the girls were still standing there. They were giggling and looking in my direction. I was so embarrassed I wanted to crawl under the table. But we both laughed at my mistake and went on to enjoy the evening.

Finally, though, the idyllic month drew toward an end. All of the experiences had steadily built confidence about the essence of my makeup and my probability for success. I was intoxicated with the excitement of the challenge before me. The artificial arm and the disabilities were now a natural part of my life, and I was in a fervor to get back into the mainstream of living.

As I reentered life, an important person left it. Grandma Ferguson, Mom's mother, died. She was buried on 27 May, my twenty-fourth birthday, at the cemetery on the edge of Covington, Indiana. Her death was especially significant because she indirectly was the reason I had enlisted in the army.

She wrote poetry, taught my brothers, sister, and me songs, and told us jokes and stories. She taught us to play cards and Monopoly. Best of all, she took us for long walks in the woods surrounding our farmhouse. Grandma and Mom were sentimentalists and their poetry, songs, and reading infected me from the moment I was born.

Grandma's letters and her last Christmas gift to me had been destroyed along with the rest of my pack when the Bouncing Betty exploded. The Christmas gift was typical of Grandma Ferguson. She had sent me a hardback copy of the

Readers' Digest Condensed Books. Although it added unnecessary weight to an already heavy pack, I continued to carry it even after I had finished all the stories. She had always given me books, and this one was my special talisman against the dangers that might come to me in Vietnam.

I stood in the only suit I owned, my army uniform, next to her grave and thought about Grandma's gift as the rain fell on the crowd while the preacher's voice intoned in the background.

Upon reflection, I figured it had done its job. The book had fallen on the trail next to me. Ugly shards of shrapnel were embedded in the shredded bulk of its pages. The book, along with other things in the pack, had absorbed the shrapnel which could have ripped into my spinal column, paralyzing me or adding just that extra bit of damage that would have killed me. I like to think that Grandma's last gift had been six hundred pages and my life.

Marshall, Illinois

Just a few days to go before my friend took me to Indianapolis where I would board the flight back to Denver. But first I wanted to make one more trip to Marshall, Illinois, to collect my thoughts and see all the places that had been so important to me. Only then would I rest easy on returning to the army hospital.

I had lived in Marshall while I was attending high school. I had many memories of those four years—of my friends, what we did, where we went, what we talked about. I was graduated from Marshall High School in 1962. From high school I went to Indiana State College at Terre Haute for three years before entering the army.

As I prowled the streets of Marshall in my Mustang, I was surprised by how little the town had changed. I think I had expected the town to have changed as much as I had. But it hadn't. Tastee-Freez at one end of town and the Dog and Suds at the other. Must have cruised back and forth between them three thousand times in four years of high school.

Yeah, my whole world used to be bounded by the perimeters of this little farming community. The nucleus was the main street, all of three blocks long. The swimming pool and fairgrounds, the Tastee-Freez, Dog and Suds, the high school: These key positions about wrapped it all up. About five miles south of town was Lincoln Trail State Park; fifteen miles north was Paris, Illinois; west of town was nothing but the highway leading out; and eighteen miles east was Terre Haute, Indiana.

I had delivered papers for Kenny Cole, the owner of the pool hall and newsstand on Main Street. I retraced the route which I had ridden my bicycle over through rain or shine or snow, weekdays, weekends, and holidays, for about two and a half years. I mentally ticked off the houses of my schoolmates on the route: Steve Etil, Gary Bosstick, Kay Lawrence, Cindy Clark, Terry Turner.

I wondered what had happened to all of them. They had been close friends once, but I had lost contact with them. What would they think of me since I lost my arm?

I pulled into the Tastee-Freez and ordered a coke from the carhop. I wanted to think about why I felt such a powerful need to return to Marshall. I was puzzled about my behavior as to why I thought there was some answer here in this town which would clarify for me the meaning of what I had gone through in Vietnam and the hospital.

I had been through a lot; I had changed so much. The only change I noticed in Marshall was that different people filled the same slots. The carhop serving me was a stranger. She had been in the third or fourth grade when my classmates had been the carhops. This girl didn't even recognize me.

This small, nondescript midwest farming community with its high school, churches, Rotary Club, Booster Club, businesses, town meetings, volunteer fire department, gas stations, three-man police department, American Legion post, and courthouse was a microcosm of what America believed itself to be.

Marshall, Illinois, represented the heart and soul of this country. The only man-made structures that jutted above the hardwood trees were church steeples, the grain elevator at the Co-op, the weather vane on the courthouse, and the water tower.

I had returned to search out the reasons I believed the way I did, and as I contemplated my life in Marshall, I began to understand that the changes I had undergone in another part of the world had had very little, if any, effect on the community I was a part of.

But the town was not supposed to change. The people changed, but not so abruptly or in such numbers as to cause discord in the community. People left slowly and others were infused slowly, causing a cumulative effect in the changing of ideas, but slowly, in pace with everything else.

This, then, was the town of America's consciousness and the reason for America's success as a stable, conservative, yet dynamic society. There was room for growth and ideas, but if any of these were abrasive, then the person who proposed them was free to move on, to another segment of American life where those particular ideas were more readily accepted.

The idea was coming to me that I had been wrong in my perspective. I had gone halfway around the world where a war was in progress, gotten myself blown to pieces, had my way of thinking altered, and, when I returned expecting dramatic changes to have also occurred at home, I had been surprised to find the attitude "Yes, it's terrible what happened to you, Freddie; and by God, what do you think we are doing fighting over there; but don't you know if this rain doesn't let up (have you heard this is the rainiest May we've had in years according to the Farmers Almanac), the farmers are going to be late getting into the fields!''

At first this seemed thoughtless, but then I realized that people were willing to help me all they could, until I either made it on my own or sank into self-pity and despair. Whatever happened, they would have completed their obligation to me as a returning soldier.

By God, it struck me, this was okay with me. I was ready to take up my obligation and be responsible for my own actions again.

This in fact was the answer I had been trying to puzzle out.

A man had to contribute himself to some purpose in his society. That was his obligation for being a member. How he did it and how effective he was weren't as important as recognizing his obligation.

An individual made a difference whether he was the president, or one of the soldiers in the war, or one of the newscasters, or a member of this town. Each one of us is important! In combat I was important to a platoon for their very lives. Presently, I was a convalescing soldier important only to family and friends. ''What would my importance be for the future,'' I wondered. I was eager to find out.

CHAPTER 7
Return to Fitzsimmons
June 1968

Boarding the aircraft at Indianapolis for the flight to Colorado was not easy. I wanted to stay here a while longer. Still ridden with doubt, in the embryo stage of my newly developed confidence, I realized I had a way to go before all issues were settled in my thinking. There were still doubt and questions tormenting me. Little did I know how vulnerable these really made me, especially when I returned to college, which I planned to do in the fall.

When the cab driver unloaded me at the front door of Fitzsimmons the sun was shining with the same intensity it had on 11 February, the day I had arrived in Colorado. But circumstances were better this time. I looked with a fuller appreciation at the blue sky. It had rained a record fourteen inches during May in Indiana. I hadn't seen much sun. I dragged my duffel bag in the front door and into the elevator and punched the fifth floor.

Walking back onto the ward at 5 West gave me a sensation akin to apprehension. What did they have planned for me now?

I reported to the head nurse, who didn't know what to do with me at first. While I waited for her to arrange my readmittance, I toured. My old room had some other young lieutenant in it. I stood at the door and stared in at the sleeping figure. I automatically checked off his injuries: a below-left-knee and below-left-elbow amputee. I wondered what had caused his wounds. I would have to ask him when he woke up.

After further exploration, I discovered that about half my old friends were gone and a new batch had replaced them. It was turning into a bitch of a year in Vietnam.

I also learned that I didn't want to be back here. I didn't want any more operations or pain. My body was working pretty good and didn't need any more work, I decided.

They assigned me a room and for about a week I stayed there. At least, during the day. But I was restless as hell and could see no reason to still be around the ward other than that it was familiar to me. At night, I would leave the hospital grounds and go through the Colfax Avenue gate to the In-niment Lounge across the street. I got stinking drunk every night, either with friends or by myself, and would stay until closing time. Then I would sneak back into the hospital and into my room where I always tossed and turned half the night until I would vomit up the alcohol. Afterward, I would sleep.

Wild Stuff

One morning Jan Gish told me I was to be assigned to the BOQ (bachelor officers' quarters) where the other crazy officers were living. Whatever kind of phase I was going through, they were going through it too so we might as well be together.

The life-style of the officers at the BOQ was totally unlike that of any other army group I had ever been in before or since. Except for a few doctors and regular duty officers, most of the men were in various stages of recuperating from wounds and operations. They were not quite dischargeable and yet too sick for regular duty. They were in between responsibilities. They had been in combat and were cocky as hell and only marginally controllable.

In many cases they tended to be irresponsible, because their attitude was "Fuck it, who gives a shit? What are they going to do? Send me to 'Nam?"

Perhaps it is unfair to call them totally irresponsible but they were certainly "crazy motherfuckers." And for a time, everyone was probably legitimately crazy, as they went through a burst of frenzied "living life to the extremes."

We had to go through a catharsis of emotion, both to show off our young animal exhilaration at having survived and to prove we still retained our reckless disdain of fear. Heavy drinking, fast driving, and hard partying were the hallmarks of this group. The nurses in their BOQ across the street, not in the least intimidated or terrorized by us, joined in the fun.

One time there was an all-night party in Otto Wagner's BOQ, after which the nurses and men dragged back to their BOQs. Otto had been a tank commander and his right arm had been blown off below the elbow by an RPG (rocket-propelled grenade) during an enemy attack. His tank had been destroyed but he and his men had escaped. During the course of the party, Otto had taken his prosthesis off, laid it down, and later became so drunk that he forgot about it.

The next morning Paul Marchi, who had passed out on the floor the night before, woke up and decided to clean the place out. Paul wasn't thinking very clearly when he found Otto's arm lying amid the garbage. He dimly remembered hearing that Otto was getting a new arm. This one must not be any good, since Otto had thrown it in the corner. So Paul put Otto's arm in with the rest of the trash and carried it out to the "Dipsy Dumpster."

Later, when Otto woke up around noon, Paul noticed Otto looking for something. He asked what the problem was and Otto said he couldn't find his arm. "Oh shit," Paul told him, "I threw it in the dumpster this morning!"

They both ran outside, climbed into the dumpster, and were digging through the trash when the nurses came by with a group of new nurses, fresh into the army. About this time, Otto found his arm and jumped up on the edge of the dumpster yelling, "I found my motherfucking arm!"

It was hard to tell who was the most startled, Otto standing half naked on the edge of the trash bin, or the nurses seeing this lunatic leaping out of the trash waving an arm.

There were some pretty sleazy bars along Colfax Avenue, and everyone could tell a story about them. But no one could top Percy when it came to the unbelievable. He had a unique wound that only seeing would be believing. An explosion had blasted a scattering of shrapnel into his groin. He had had an exceptionally long penis, but after numerous operations involving cutting, sewing, and grafts, it was bent at strange angles and had chunks missing. As Wagner put it, "Old Percy's dick looked like ten miles of bad road."

The doctors wanted a sperm sample to determine if Percy was sterile, but because of the damage Percy hadn't gotten an erection yet. The doctors had given Percy a specimen tube to carry around in case the time arose when Percy might get a sperm sample.

Percy was worried about his future sexual ability and so he religiously carried the specimen tube in his shirt pocket. One night when he was drunk he achieved fame at a local bar and dance hall when he convinced one of the girls to masturbate him so he could get a sperm specimen. Of course, the girls in this particular place would do anything for the right price, but Percy's fame came because he appealed to the girl's patriotic spirit and got the sperm sample for free.

Another episode occurred one night when Marchi accidentally drove Glenn's MG through the front glass of the liquor store located in the shopping area at the corner of Colfax Avenue and Peoria Street, right outside the hospital grounds.

Paul's foot had missed the brake and the MG jumped the curb and crashed through the window, stopping halfway inside the store.

When the astounded owner came out from under the counter, Glenn leaned out of the car window and said, "We would like a case of Bud to go."

One night Sam was coming back drunk from a party and he drove his big Buick into the guard shack at the Colfax entrance, knocking the shack off its foundation. The two MPs barely jumped out of the way in time.

Two weeks later, at a pool party, Roger Tiley, a Cobra helicopter gun-ship pilot, jumped into the pool. That was not so unusual, but Roger had been shot in the jaw with a .50 caliber while on a mission in Vietnam, and the lower part of his face was blown away. The doctors had spent a year and a half rebuilding his face and Roger had grafts and tubes sticking out everywhere. When he jumped into the pool the tube in his stomach and the tube at the base of his throat came out and Roger started filling up with water.

Everyone jumped to the rescue and someone said that Roger had to go to the hospital quick. They loaded him into the back seat of Sam's Buick and piled in while Sam got the car started. Unfortunately, Sam was drunk again and as he wove toward the Colfax entrance at a high rate of speed, the MPs recognized the car and from a protected area waved them to a halt. They all piled out of the car and started talking at once. They told the MPs to look in the back seat.

When they did, one of the guys holding a finger over the hole where the tubes used to be took his finger away and water actually dribbled out. One of the MPs threw up, but Roger just lay there smiling.

One night Captain Paolo Marchi was throwing a party in his BOQ apartment located a few blocks from Fitzsimmons.

No one called him Paolo. His name was Paul or Marchi or "the Wop" or a combination of those, depending on the status of the person addressing him.

Paul had been shot five or six times with an AK-47. All of his parts were still attached, but the damage done to nerve, muscle, and other tissues interfered with how well those parts worked.

As he and I got to talking one night, we discovered we had met briefly in Vietnam, when his platoon relieved mine in October 1967 at bridges 101, 102, and 103 a few kilometers south of Duc Pho. I had taken Delta 1–6 out for one last night ambush the evening of the day his platoon took responsibility for the bridges. The next day when we returned to the bridges after a successful ambush, he and I had shaken hands and parted, never expecting to meet again.

Unlike me, Paul had mastered the art of evading work therapy details, especially the "death officer" job. His philosophy was simple: "If they can't find me, they can't assign me." He was assisted in this evasion by one of his friends assigned to the work therapy office.

The powers that be, however, had been zeroing in. They were coming so close to nailing Paul that he had stopped answering the phone in his apartment. He always had his roommate or a friend answer. If the caller sounded official, his instructions were to report that Paul was at Fitzsimmons on his way to physical therapy, actually in it, or on the way back.

This worked for a while, until the work therapy group became so persistent in its pursuit that Paul put the telephone in the refrigerator.

Everything hummed along until, at one of his parties lasting well into the wee hours, Paul went to the refrigerator for a beer, feeling no pain. As he bent over with his hand stuck partway inside, rummaging through the refrigerator, the telephone on the second shelf started to ring. Half in a stupor, Paul jumped, banging his head on the freezer door. He backed away swearing and rubbing the knot on his head. The phone continued to ring.

The combination of the hour, the alcohol, and the knot on his head must have dulled Paul's thinking because he reached into the refrigerator and picked up the telephone receiver. The conversation went something like this:

"Is this Captain Marchi?" the voice asked.

"Uh, yeah, what you want?"

"This is Lieutenant Jones, officer of the day at Fitzsimmons, and I am assigning you to be escort officer for a body arriving at Buckley Field at 1000 hours today. You are to report in here at 0800 hours in full-dress uniform and packed for a three-day trip."

"Oh shit." Paul's worst nightmare had come true, but army life had made him light on his feet. "Lieutenant Jones! You are talking to a captain and a captain in the infantry does not receive orders from a lieutenant. I am therefore ordering you, lieutenant, to assume the duties as escort officer and to conduct yourself accordingly. You are dismissed!" Paul hung up and slammed the refrigerator door.

"Goddamn, they about got me," he remarked.

At 0810, there was a fierce hammering at the door. The party had wound down to the hard-core. When Paul opened the door, he was confronted by a very angry lieutenant colonel flanked by two big, mean-looking MPs.

"Captain Marchi! Stand at attention! I am a colonel, as you can see; therefore, I outrank you. You will report in full-dress uniform to the orderly room in forty-five minutes. You will act as escort officer on this assignment and you will meet the aircraft arriving at Buckley at 1000 hours. You had better be standing tall."

"Yes, sir."

"When you return I will decide whether you will be court-martialed or not! I do not appreciate the crap you wounded officers are allowed to get away with. Perhaps I should make an example out of you, Captain. You guys may think you are heroes but you are still in the army and therefore will follow orders, or do you want to be discharged as a private, Captain Marchi?"

"No, sir."

"All right then, you have forty minutes to report. I suggest you move it!" The colonel closed the door with Paul still standing at attention.

Smiling, Paul turned to the group. "I knew I should have had the fucking phone taken out. Well, see you guys." He ran into the bathroom and turned on the shower.

These escapades were part of our journey home. Thousands of men went through Fitzsimmons, and every one of them had some opportunity to behave extravagantly. Most did so in varying degrees.

Neither the war nor the results of war were far from us: There were our increasing awareness of anti-war sentiment, the nightly newscasts, the steady stream of casualties into the hospitals, and the too frequent notice of a friend who had been wounded or killed. Indeed, the permanent residue of our own wounds would forever keep the war near.

Yes, we thought we had good reason to get drunk and act crazy. Some reasons were more powerful reinforcers than others for doing what we did.

From it all we gained strength, though at times we were pushed to our individual limits. Even the wounded still had their duty.

My worst time came early on and required a great sense of duty. It involved one of the jobs we all dreaded: the task of death officer.

The Dying Sergeant

Jesus Christ! How did I get picked for this job? I thought for the hundredth time. Work therapy had some shitty details but the implications of this particular job were staggering to me.

I checked myself out in the full-length mirror fastened to the wall outside my room in the BOQ. I was in my dress greens, complete with medals. I had to look perfect for what I was going to do. Satisfied with my appearance, I walked through the living room where other officers were watching TV.

I hadn't been in the BOQ long enough to know the other guys very well. The little I did know was that they were masters at avoiding work therapy duties. I wasn't, which was why I was in dress uniform when the other guys were drinking beer and yelling encouragement to me as I went to do my duty.

The army's theory was to put a soldier to work as soon as he was able to perform some function. There were many valid reasons for work therapy: Work provided an outlet for energy to relieve boredom, encouraged the soldier in his re-habilitation, gave him a purpose and responsibility each day, and helped the army to fill some of its pressing manpower needs. As with any organization, there were never enough people to do all the tasks that needed to be done.

This is especially true of military organizations during a war. With all of the things waiting to be done, the army wisely decided that there was no sense in having all these wounded men sitting around doing nothing when putting them to work would be beneficial for everybody.

Not all of the men agreed with that philosophy. They felt they had already done enough for their country. Their at-titude was, "What's the big idea putting a wounded guy to work? Gimme a break!"

When I received orders to report for work therapy soon after I was put on out-patient status, I know I was sure surprised to hear the officers in charge tell me I had to start working. I had assumed I would be a patient until the hospital dismissed me, whereupon I would be assigned to an army unit.

Of course, a hospital the size of Fitzsimmons was of itself an army unit. It had everything from MPs at the gate to an eighteen-hole golf course.

There was another factor I had to face up to. I was no longer assigned as a platoon leader in Delta Company, First of the Fourteenth, Third Brigade, Fourth Division, Vietnam. My status and unit had officially been changed to that of a patient at Fitzsimmons Army Hospital, Colorado, U.S.A., some time ago. Even so I had not allowed myself to believe completely that I had been discontinued as a member of Delta Company.

Walking along the sidewalk toward the main hospital in the early evening of a Colorado spring, I admitted that I had known the answer a long time ago: When a man was wounded he was carried on the company rolls until the first sergeant was notified that the man was unable to return. Only then was his name removed from the company duty roster.

I had identified so strongly with my platoon and company that at times during my hospitalization only the strength of the bond between us kept me going. I hated the thought of my name being removed from the rolls. But it had been and I was now a part of this army unit, Fitzsimmons Hospital. Now my duty was here. I kept reminding myself that someone had to do the tough jobs and it might as well be the infantry.

I pushed open the back doors of the hospital and walked over to the elevator bank where I pushed the button for the correct floor. "Sometimes the army asks too much of me," I thought in self-pity.

* * *

My duty tonight was to meet at 2000 hours with the family
of a sergeant who was terminally ill from an exotic tropical
disease. Very little was known about the disease other than
that it was contracted in the Far East, seemed to hit men in
their thirties and forties, and slowly attacked the nervous
system, irreversibly destroying it. The symptoms would not
show up until months after the disease struck. This sergeant
had been to Vietnam, finished his tour, and served in Germany with his wife almost a year before the disease started
showing itself. When the army doctors couldn't figure out
what was wrong, he had been sent back to the States for
study and better care. But nothing seemed to stop it. The disease caused increasing paralysis, making the patient pro-
gressively more helpless until in the final stages he could do
nothing for himself. He could at the last only move his eyelids in response to questions, until even that function failed
and the eyes stared straight ahead. No one knew if he was
aware of his existence during this stage or not. The next step
was death.

My orders were to explain to the dependents in the presence of the sergeant the details of the benefits available to
them in life insurance payments, widow's pension, medical
care, and other things they needed to know. This included
burial benefits and burial details such as where they wished
to have the funeral and how he was to be buried.

The army meant no harm. The army in fact prided itself
on "taking care of its own." It was the carrying out of that
intent that at times left something to be desired. This was
duty calling for an experienced officer but no one wanted
that kind of duty. Consequently, young officers who were
healing and were not part of the regular staff were invariably
chosen.

I had prepared myself as well as I could with the information given to me to study. How I actually imparted the
knowledge was left up to me. The sergeant who had given

me the packet had no advice, nor did the captain and the major who were in charge of the duty assignments and were themselves recuperating from wounds. They advised me to dress in full uniform and to do the best I could. The family had been notified and would meet me in the dying sergeant's room at 2000 hours. I was on my own. I thought back on the conversation earlier in the day in the officers' work therapy office in Building T-809.

"You're hard-core infantry, Downs. You can handle it," the captain kidded me.

When I walked into his hospital room, his wife and her parents were standing. They turned to me; the air was electric.

This sergeant might die at any moment. After months of long struggle, the disease had backed him into the last corner where death was waiting. His family had been with him through those long months of struggle. They had seen him deteriorate from the robust and vibrant man they loved into a zombie who now lay dying. Their shared hopes and dreams had deteriorated along with the man until now the only thing left common to them all was love and remorse. And, unbeknownst to me, an undefinable hatred for the system which had brought about these circumstances.

As I faced the dying sergeant's wife and her parents across the room, I knew very well that I romanticized most things in life, including the army. But in coming to grips with life, I still needed to draw strength from the ideal of a thing.

The room was small. A narrow, high, steel-framed hospital bed with cranks to adjust the mattress was in the middle of the floor. Enough space was around all sides of the bed to allow free movement. The doors to the bathroom and closet were along a wall. The walls were a light cream; the floor was made of white foot-square tiles. On the wall opposite the door was a window. It was dark outside but I knew from the location of the room that the view through the window would have shown the tops of the trees and tops of the buildings behind the hospital: housing, administration, commissary, the P.X., library, barbershop, and others. Towering above the buildings and trees would be the solitary red and white checkered water tower, over by the golf course.

The view out of the window was important to me, especially now that I was in the room with the sergeant. When I was lying in the bed I occupied for three months, I had basically the same view. I knew the tops of those trees and buildings perfectly. Knowing what was outside the window helped me now in some unmeasurable way. I looked at the sergeant lying flat, his thin body barely profiled under the white sheet, his hazel eyes staring straight up.

I grasped in all directions, but there were no more handles: I, too, was committed to finishing this out. The sergeant was a soldier as I was. I turned toward the family.

"Good evening, I'm Lieutenant Frederick Downs, Jr. I'm pleased to meet you." I shook hands with the old man. It seemed to me he took pleasure in discovering I had no grip with my weak hand.

I invited them to sit but they refused. I stood next to the bed on the sergeant's left side. His wife stood at the foot. We looked at each other across the corner of the bed. She was a slight woman in her early thirties and dressed very nicely in a mild plaid suit with a white blouse. She carried herself well.

She stood unmoving, staring directly at me. Her parents stood behind her, off to her left. All listened impassively to what I was saying to the sergeant's wife. I was trying very hard to do this correctly. As I read from my notes fastened to the small clipboard that was in the case I carried my papers in, I hoped he was proud of me and that I was representing the army the way he would have expected. I felt a strong affinity with this man who was a "lifer."

I finished one section and was going on to the next section

when a snarl exploded from his wife's throat. She took two steps toward me and swung her open hand against my face. I was stunned. I felt my face flush from both the blow and the surprise. I stepped partially back as she followed through with another blow from her other hand. I was forced back against the wall as she hammered at my face in a frenzy of blows.

I was embarrassed, afraid, befuddled. She was hurting me, yet I couldn't swing back at a woman. I tried to put my arms up to protect myself, but my artificial arm wouldn't come unlocked. I held my right arm in front of my face to ward off her blows.

"Jesus, lady, stop! Please stop! What did I do? You're hurting me. Quit." I cried out. Her blows were hurting my arm where many of the wounds were taking the force of her fists. I wanted to be brave and stand like a man while she spent herself, but I could not. She was hurting me. I was against the wall with my arm up when a burst of agonizing pain from my arm caused me to suck in my breath.

I cried out in pain and fear. This was my only arm and it didn't work very well. I was terrified something bad had happened to my arm. My cry startled her, checking the blows. She backed away. I kept my arm up because to move it sent waves of nauseating pain to my stomach. I wanted to vomit. Blood seeped through the uniform sleeve near the elbow. The bright red blood dripped down the front of my dress green uniform.

I was crying, sobbing, coming unglued. Tears ran down my face from hurt and rage. Within my whole body, violence was thrashing wildly about, trying to form an exit.

I hated myself for being so foolish with my romantic thoughts of the army, death, war, pain, and everything else in this world. The sergeant was probably a malingerer; this bitch was probably fucking around and couldn't wait to get the insurance money; I was only twenty-four years old and

I didn't know what I was doing here. The army didn't care about anybody and I was a fool to think I was anything but cannon fodder and a pawn. Rich people's kids didn't go to war; they went to college and made fun of us dummies.

I'll show them. I'll show them all, the motherfuckers. I have killed better people than these scumbags.

I was beginning to feel the giddy aftermath of conflict when the girl finally stopped crying long enough to tell me she was sorry. She and parents apologized profusely, explaining it was not me personally or anything I did, but just the strain, blah blah blah. . . .

I couldn't care less by now. I had retreated to isolation. I told them I was okay, the blood would wash out, and could we please finish up so I could go get bandaged?

The parents picked up my case file and papers and put them on the bed for me. Moving painfully, I sorted the papers back into order and finished what I had been sent to do. Through it all the sergeant had lain immobile, unable to respond to the storm or to the calm that followed.

We left the room and, while walking down the hall, I realized I had forgotten my cap. I bid them goodbye and went back. My cap was on the floor next to the window. I was in a lot of pain and had talked the night nurse into giving me three Darvons. I added another one I had stashed in my pocket, but even the four of them didn't help when I leaned down to pick up the cap. The pain was terrible. I retrieved the cap, stuck it on my head, and stared out the window at the lights.

I moved over to the bed, looking down into the sergeant's eyes, remembering Yoder, one of my men who had been killed in an ambush on 22 November 1967. After the fight we had put the bodies of the dead men next to a landing zone hacked out of a ridge up in the jungle. While waiting for the dust-off to come in for the dead and wounded, I had gone over to Yoder's body. I remembered what I had thought at the time.

"Man's beginning and man's end would always be attended by only a few. Those that bore him at birth and those that bore him at death."

I had saluted Yoder as his body lay sprawled out on the jungle floor. It was a private thing between him and me. Probably others who hadn't been through a lot of shit wouldn't comprehend such a gesture and would perceive a salute as melodramatic, but I had been honoring his passing in the only way I understood.

In the quiet of the dying sergeant's room with the earlier emotions still fresh in my mind, I wondered what happened to a man when he let life beat him down until he no longer believed in dreams. Would it happen to me?

I leaned over to make sure I was in the sergeant's line of sight. As I saluted him, a drop of blood fell from my sleeve.

A nurse friend in 5 West rebandaged my arm. I walked over to the officers' club where I sat by myself and drank whiskey until my memories faded for the night.

CHAPTER 8
Welcome Back
Summer 1968

The summer sped along in a stop-frame of experiences intensified by the potency of the emotions we ranged through. Some of the men faltered from the strain but for the majority the tribulations made us stronger.

We had been violently thrust together and at first we were held by the common bond of our wounds, the hospital, and the war. But our independent personalities caused the bond to dissolve, in the natural course of things, as we acted on the decisions necessary to start our new life patterns. The bond was never meant to be permanent. Healthy friendships would develop, but that would involve a different bonding process altogether.

The hospital environment for a patient was an artificial one for normal living. It was only a way station to be used during an emergency. The hospital's function was accomplished as soon as our physical crises were past, because we were now in good enough shape to continue on our way.

Which way we were to go was a common topic in the bull sessions held in the BOQ and the bars where we hung out: stay in the army, get out, go to college, return home, travel, be a bum; we discussed it all.

This was a rare opportunity. We were free to start any new life we chose.

Personally, my plans for an army career did not look so

hot. I could stay in under the "whole-man" concept in which they allowed disabled soldiers to remain in the army, but after hard deliberation I decided that my army career was over.

I turned down the surgeon's offer to operate on my arm to make it work better. I told them I would get by. Consequently my reasons for staying at the hospital faded away. I asked around and was told that the army would allow me to attend school in the fall even though I would not be officially discharged until 1969.

This sounded like a good deal to me so I applied to the University of Denver, a "rich kid's" private college. The representative from the Veterans Administration had explained that I was eligible for the vocational rehabilitation program, which meant that all tuitions and fees would be paid to any college which would accept me. This was like a dream come true.

I took the entrance tests the university required and wrote to my college counselor at Indiana State University asking for a letter of reference.

There was other good news. I was informed by the Army Physical Evaluation Board that I would be eligible for a monthly pension the rest of my life. This was to be paid on the disabilities incurred in combat. I was stupefied at this news. Also, I was a little embarrassed to know I would be receiving money from the government. I was still very naive about government social obligations.

The implications of this forthcoming money took an enormous burden from me. I now remembered that people along the way had informed me that I would receive compensation from the government but I had been so wrapped up in the pain and drugs, coping from day to day with more immediate problems, that that piece of information had not sunk in.

Now I would never have to worry about becoming destitute if my disability kept me from working. This cheered me considerably, although, in truth, I could never imagine my not being able to do something to earn a living, disability or not.

So much good news came to me during the summer of 1968. And changes in my life were occurring. It was an exciting time.

One of the seeds for a major change in my life had been unsuspectingly planted in an innocent encounter soon after my return from Indianapolis. It had happened on a typical evening when we had started drinking at the Beachhead. At the time I never dreamed what that evening would lead to. It began in good infantry style.

Talk at the Beachhead

The officers' club at Fitzsimmons had a dress code even in the off hours. None of us in the BOQ liked this formality since we were young officers on out-patient status with few good clothes, marking time while our wounds healed. The truth is, we didn't fit in with the older officers anyhow. Most of them were noncombat, not real army to us. And we were heavy drinkers with a tendency to get rowdy and not care much who noticed because there wasn't a Goddamn thing anybody could do to us that was worse than what we had already been through.

The army in its long history of dealing with healing young men was prepared to let us burn off some of the "piss and vinegar."

At Fitzsimmons the solution for guys like us was a bar called the Beachhead, set up in a building next to the officers' club. It was at the Beachhead that we would meet in the late afternoon after work detail or physical therapy to plan the evening. Many times we sallied forth having drunk so much booze that we provided our own entertainment.

One day late in the week as I sat with two of my friends, Ron, a major who had lost one leg below the knee from a grenade explosion, and Jim, a captain who had been shot in the stomach, our favorite subject arose.

"Pussy! What I wouldn't give for a nice piece of ass right now," Jim slouched back in his chair and took a drink from his glass of bourbon and soda.

"Fucking A. Would you believe it's been so long since I've had a piece I think I've forgotten when it was," I agreed. Tipping back on my chair I lit a cigarette and practiced holding it in my hook while I used the other to hold the bourbon and coke I was drinking.

Ron got up to punch a few buttons on the jukebox and then returned to our table. He shook a cigarette out of a pack lying on the table. I practiced using my hook to give him a light.

"Getting pretty good with that, Lieutenant. Chipped any more teeth lately?"

Everybody cracked up.

"Very fucking funny. You should be shot for making fun of the handicapped. Besides, you're avoiding the real issue here. You know some decent pussy or not?"

"Yeah, that's right Downs, old Ronnie here is avoiding the question. Are you shitting us or you got some stuff stashed away, Ronnie?"

"You know what I think, Jim?"

"What, Downs?"

"I think the major is dinky-dow. He doesn't have a woman." I looked at Ron across the table. "What woman would want to go out with a one-legged major with an artificial leg?"

Jim and I winked at each other. Sure we had called the major's bluff. All of us talked about pussy so much but yet saw so little of it that we were used to lying to each other.

"Except a one-legged woman!" Ron challenged us across the table.

There was a moment of silence while Jim and I digested this bit of shocking news.

"Of course!" Jim said in awe.

"A one-legged woman. Why didn't we think of that, Jim?" I turned to Jim with an exaggerated rolling of my eyes.

"And we'll get a one-armed woman for you, Downs," Jim said as he slapped me on the back.

"How about a woman with two bellybuttons for you, Jim? That's as good as a bullet hole." I started laughing.

"A one-eyed broad for John and for Mike we can get a crazy woman."

"Hell yes, the possibilities are endless. Why didn't we think of this before, Jim?"

"Only a major could think this good. A sure sign of a lifer officer. This man is destined for general's stars without a doubt!"

"How about it, Major, does your one-legged girl have a one-armed friend and another friend with two bellybuttons? Man, we are hot to go!"

"Listen, Ron, you really got a one-legged girl?"

"Hummm, bet you met her on that amputee skiing program I heard about. Does she ski?"

"Yeah, she skis damn good. You may have read about her. Her name is Jan. She lost a leg. Cancer."

"Is that right? A whole leg? And she skis. Shiiit, I couldn't do that."

"Forget the skiing. Does she have two friends?"

"She's got two roommates but I don't think they are interested in meeting anybody. One works for the FBI and the other one is an older, no-nonsense type."

"We don't care, let's give it a try. Anything beats sitting around here drinking by ourselves. Give this Jan a call and see if the three of them would like to go out for a drink."

"Or dinner. We'll even take them out to dinner."

"With what, dummy. You got any money?"

"Would you believe, I don't have any money? Scratch the dinner."

"What are you waiting for? Here's a dime, make the call, time is wasting!"

Jim and I sat drinking while Ron made the phone call at the pay phone near the entrance. We eagerly waited for his return. This long shot was too improbable and we had resigned ourselves to getting drunk again at the bar across from the main gate on Colfax. The Inniment Lounge was our second home by now.

Ron returned and sat down. "Okay, I got you lined up; sort of."

"What? That's fucking outstanding!"

"Sort of? What do you mean, sort of?"

"I talked Jan into letting us come over, but she hasn't exactly told the other two we're coming. I told her we would bring a case of beer."

"Ooohhh, candy's dandy, but liquor's quicker." Jim rubbed his hands together.

"Good thing she didn't ask them, that way they don't have a chance to turn us down. Let's go quick, before something bad happens and they take off."

As Ron drove down Colfax toward Denver, he issued instructions. "These girls live in a house. They are nice so don't be swearing and saying 'fuck' or they'll throw us out."

"Can we say 'fornicate' instead?"

"Will you shut the fuck up, Downs. I'm serious. Now let me finish. Jim, you get the FBI girl and, Fred, you are the lowest ranking officer so you get stuck with the other one."

"You mean the no-nonsense one?"

"Yeah, don't be surprised if she just up and leaves while you're talking. She's like that if she decides she doesn't like you."

"Sounds like it's a fucking lick on me. At least I'll have plenty of beer to drink."

When we arrived with the case of beer at the front door of the one-story brick house near the intersection of Colorado Boulevard and Colfax, it was obvious that we had not been expected by anyone other than Jan.

Not to be deterred by so trivial a problem we acted like invited guests while Jan introduced us. The case of beer was put into the refrigerator and then we were steered to our respective places.

I was seated next to Mary, "the other one," who was sitting on the living room couch with a friend of hers, David.

Oh, what a tough evening for me. I felt very much out of place with this lady. She had a college degree and her parents owned a business. She talked about classical music and literature, both of which were out of my range.

Finally her friend, David, got up to leave, which gave me an opportunity to talk about something I knew. David was riding a scooter and since I had once owned and raced motorcycles, I was able to hold up my end of the conversation while I checked out his vehicle.

Toward the end of the evening, what with the beer, I was feeling much more confident and was describing to Mary how my arm worked. I told her I could do practically anything with it and to prove this I would open another can of beer.

I had been opening beer ever since being fitted with the hook, so I sure didn't anticipate any difficulty this time.

I stood in the doorway between the kitchen and dining room holding the sixteen-ounce can of Coors and my hook worked perfectly but my hand slipped and the can dropped to the floor.

Coors beer exploded out of the can onto the ceiling, spraying both Mary and me.

"Oh fuck," I said to myself.

Everyone stopped talking. Beer was dripping off the ceiling on Mary. I couldn't think of anything funny to say and she did not seem amused.

"Well, on to the next can," I quipped, rather limp, but in the best tradition of the infantry, which was to keep going. Somehow we worked out of it and when Ron, Jim, and I decided to go, I stood at the doorway and as a matter of courtesy told Mary I would call her some time, perhaps we'd have dinner. I figured this woman was definitely not interested in seeing me again, but she surprised me by saying she would be happy to go out.

As the three of us rode up Colfax in the Cougar, I opened beer for us from the remnants of the case.

"Sure know how to fuck up, don't you, Downs?"

"You guys never dropped a can of beer before?"

"Hell yes, but not on a first date, for Christ's sake!"

I took a long swig. "It's a lick on me. That woman won't let me near the place now."

"Goddamn Downs, you were funny. If you could have seen yourself with that beer dripping onto your head. You looked like you had just swallowed a dog turd."

"I felt like it, too. Goddamn, did I feel dumb. Oh well, fuck it! Let's go to the Inniment."

"Great idea. Can't take any of this shit seriously, it'll kill you."

More of my bravado. Actually I had been fascinated by Mary but did not intend to call her. No matter how confident I thought I was, I did not want the humiliation of being turned down for a date. Even more abhorrent to me was the belief that she was too much a lady to turn me down outright but might accept a date with me out of pity. I sure as hell didn't want a woman to date me because she felt sorry for me. I wasn't that brave yet.

I need not have worried. She didn't wait for my call—

she called me. After I got over my pleasant surprise we agreed to a dinner date and after that we began to date regularly.

I often wondered what her friends thought of me and my friends. We were, without a doubt, in different leagues.

The Soft Touch

Andy and I were on a double date with Mary and a friend of hers, Judy, who had just flown in from England. Andy, a captain, was on work therapy at the Rocky Mountain Arsenal. The army stored nerve gas out there in the prairie northeast of Denver's airport, Stapleton International, and needed officers to assist in the administrative work. To help them out, Fitzsimmons would assign officers on work therapy to the arsenal.

Andy was about six feet tall with a light build. He had been shot in the head, the bullet knocking out a chunk of skull but doing very little brain damage. At least none that we could tell. He didn't act any crazier than the rest of us.

We had gone to dinner at a good restaurant and later in the evening had stopped at a place we knew had a dance band. A "high-class joint" the guys back at the Beachhead would have dubbed it.

Andy and I were feeling rowdy. This was caused in part by the booze and the company of women, but we knew we were supposed to make a good impression so we refrained from being loud and, instead, we channeled our rowdiness into talk about the war—our perennial subject. Finally we came around to the one part of the war that had brought us together—our wounds.

The girls always seemed as fascinated by our wounds as they were appalled at the brutality of the war itself. This did not surprise us because they were no more fascinated with our wounds than we were.

We loved to brag about how we had gotten hit. We always tried to act like it was nothing and the wound didn't slow us down a bit.

The more horrible the conditions surrounding the time we were wounded and the greater the difficulty we faced during the evacuation, the better we liked telling the story.

We liked it now but our stories, all still true at this stage, were a bravado we used to keep outsiders in awe of our ordeals in war, wounds, and healing. We did not tell the stories to impress them; quite the contrary—we ourselves were in awe of what we had gone through and survived.

We spent hours discussing among ourselves what we had endured in combat. Our experiences were unique because of the nature of our work—to kill men whose job it was to kill us. The telling of the stories became almost a tribal ritual.

At first, time would be our friend. Each day that passed eroded some of the memory of the pain. In ten or fifteen years the pain would slowly return as old shrapnel, old wounds, and occasionally bad memories would remind us how aging had been speeded up in proportion to the magnitude of wounds received in our youth.

But that was to be. Now we laughed a lot, drank too much, drove too fast, chain-smoked, and wrung what we could out of life.

Judy asked Andy, "How did you get wounded?"

"I got shot in the head," Andy smiled.

"What kind of damage did you sustain? Has it affected you any?" The idea of surviving a bullet to the head seemed impossible.

Andy leaned forward and put his finger to his head. "The bullet blew a piece of the skull out; here, feel the soft spot. That's where it hit."

"Soft spot! You mean there isn't a steel plate to protect

the brain?" Judy asked in astonishment as she and Mary gingerly rested a finger on the spot Andy indicated.

After their examination Andy sat back and swallowed the rest of his drink. He ordered another round.

"Nope," Andy replied. "The doctors can't put a plate in because they're not sure all of the danger of infection is past. Isn't it something like that, Fred?"

"Yeah, they're afraid your brain will start swelling, I think."

Judy, who had a Ph.D. in pharmacology with an emphasis on chemical reaction in the brain, looked perplexed. "If that is true shouldn't you be taking medicine of some sort?"

"Oh, I am taking medicine to keep from having seizures," Andy said as he picked up the drink the waitress had just delivered.

Mary, who was thinking along the same lines as Judy, asked specifically, "If you're taking medicine to control seizures then you shouldn't be drinking, should you?"

With a perplexed look on his face, Andy looked at me and then at the girls. A mischievous grin spread over his face. "You're right, I'm not supposed to be drinking. This stuff could kill me. Right, Fred?"

"Yep, that's what they say."

"Well, it's a short life, but a merry one," and so saying he took another drink while the girls looked aghast, expecting Andy to drop dead right there at the table.

We had a lot of fun doing things like that. It was even more fun when we returned to the BOQ with stories for the guys about how we had shocked the ladies. This behavior was normal for us at the time, but it was coming to a close for me.

A Retirement Parade

It was the end of summer and my time of craziness was over. An era was passing for me. I was still assigned to the hospital but, spiritually, I was elsewhere.

By coincidence, General Blunt, the commander at Fitzsimmons, decided to retire. He was a good man and was well liked by his staff. He took pride in his hospital so his staff arranged to have some of the wounded officers and enlisted men from the medical holding company formed into a platoon. They were to march in review with the regular unit platoons and companies on the day of his retirement.

Captain Smith was chosen as company commander, and I was chosen as platoon leader. Smith's right arm was a flail, shot by an enemy sniper bullet. I was wearing an artificial arm, and the platoon sergeant had a mangled leg. Every man in our medical holding platoon was wounded in some fashion. Some had an eye missing or a face wound, others limped from leg injuries, a couple had arms or hands missing. We called ourselves the Invalid Brigade.

But we were standing tall in our summer khaki uniforms and black spit-shined shoes. We knew we were the best soldiers in the army. We also knew that this would probably be our last military formation.

On the appointed day in the early afternoon, Captain Smith marched us into our assigned positions at the end of a long, orderly line of companies and platoons standing to our right in orderly ranks and rows across the back of the parade field.

The artillery guns used to fire the salutes stood to our left only a few meters away. A military band stood playing in the middle of the field.

I could see across the expanse of carefully tended lush green grass the small reviewing stand where the generals stood. A set of bleachers was alongside the reviewing stand.

They were crowded with staff, family, and friends. A group of people who did not have seats stood alongside the field next to the bleachers.

Behind the crowd I could see the end of my BOQ building.

Tall elm trees were spaced evenly, completely around the border of the parade field. The officers' club was at the north end.

I thought about the tableau of which I was a part. This small retirement ceremony was the type repeated at army bases around the world. It was the best kind it seemed to me—only the people who care were involved.

The ceremony was coming to a close. Orders were bellowed across the parade field to the company commander, who repeated them to the platoon leaders, who repeated them to the platoon.

We were called to attention and to present arms.

Each time the guns thundered a salute, we would involuntarily flinch, our leg muscles tightening, causing us to bob up and down in cadence with the cannon.

Finally that was over and the band marched to the other end of the field to lead the companies and platoons past the reviewing stand. Each company in turn peeled away to follow the preceding company around the parade field to pass in review before the general.

We were the last in line. When it came our turn we marched the length of the field along the back edge; the band was standing in formation next to the reviewing stand, playing so that each unit would be in step when it passed the general. The brassy notes came across the field to us. The order "column left" was given to me by Captain Smith, which I repeated to the troops marching in step behind me.

I strode briskly: The sunshine, the grass underfoot, the breeze across the field, the music, the crowds, and the men all around me combined to provide me with a sense of pride of all that I had accomplished in the army. It had all cost so much, taken so much effort, and changed me in so many ways.

I felt a pang of regret that my tour was ending.

We came to the corner of the field; Captain Smith ordered "column left," which I repeated, and we turned.

We marched down the last stretch. As we came close to the reviewing stand I saw from the corner of my eye the men, women, and children in the bleachers rise to their feet. They began to applaud our platoon of wounded men. They continued to applaud as we marched by.

As the order to "present arms" was given and we passed by in review of the generals, tears welled up in my eyes at the display of respect shown to us.

The thought sprang to mind that I had finally had my welcoming home band.

It had been a long time coming.

Epilogue:
A Soldier's Return

Shortly after the parade I received notice that I had been accepted as a probationary student at the University of Denver. To complete my good fortune and joy in the waning days of summer, Mary and I decided to become engaged.

We were married in September in Big Elk Meadows, a small stream-fed valley in the Rocky Mountains near Estes Park, Colorado. It was eleven o'clock in the morning when, under a deep sapphire sky, we stood in her mother's yard in the meadow while the preacher conducted the private ceremony.

White cumulus clouds drifted majestically through the sky. The gray, rugged mountain peaks were outlined starkly against the blue sky. A green mantle of pines, aspen, and grasses covered the mountain slopes and ridges.

I admired the beauty of the peaceful setting on the stage beginning a new chapter in my life. One year ago I had stepped off the aircraft onto the soil of Vietnam.

That first step off the plane had been the start of the longest year in my life. I breathed deeply at the memories: Now I was done with the war, the year was over, Vietnam was behind me.

. . . But I was wrong. Vietnam was poisoning the soul of

America. I was to find that Vietnam would permeate my life far beyond the physical damage of my body.

The soldiers of Vietnam entered a limbo for years. Caused by a misperception of their role, they would be miscast as the villains in the historical morality play of America versus Vietnam.

An early, bizarre example set the stage for what was to come. The story, although strange, was repeated many times in various formats in the years to follow, especially in college.

Other soldiers will recognize this story, but civilians will find it hard to believe.

The Wedding Photograph: September 1968

We had not had formal pictures taken during the wedding. Now, two weeks later, we were dressing up again in our wedding clothes to have pictures taken for the future.

I was in our bedroom, standing in front of the mirror, surveying my army dress greens—immaculate, freshly cleaned and pressed, silver first lieutenant's bars on the epaulet, Fourth Division ivy patch on the left shoulder, name tag "Downs" above the right chest pocket, three rows of medals on the left chest pocket. Above the medals was the combat infantryman's badge (CIG), a frontier rifle surrounded by a wreath signifying that it had been earned in combat.

I looked at my face, measuring the past with the present. My body was filling out rapidly now. From one hundred seventy pounds in Vietnam to one hundred twenty pounds in the hospital and back up to one hundred forty pounds. My uniform was still a little loose on my frame but I liked the look of it on me.

Damn! I was proud to be an infantry soldier in the United

States Army. I hated leaving the service, but in a few months, on 1 January 1969, I would be medically discharged after having served three years. It had been one hell of an experience.

When everything was said and done, it was the infantry that fought the enemy where it counted most, in the dirt and mud, killing or being killed.

I was proud to have fought for my country and even willing to do it again. I was in fact very happy. The euphoria of having beside me a beautiful new wife whom I loved and admired blended perfectly with my feelings of being gloriously alive with the promise of the new future.

I carefully put my cap on my head, pulled the shiny black bill down two fingers' width above my nose, stood at attention and saluted myself.

"Pretty bad," I thought. "My hand and arm are twisted too much from the scar tissue. Hell, what difference does it make; I feel good and if someone doesn't like my salute what are they going to do? Send me to 'Nam?" I smiled at the old refrain.

The photography shop was downtown. We walked into the studio to be greeted by the owner, a man my size only heavier, his face lined by wrinkles, his hair receding, and an old man's paunch pushing his belt out. He came around a counter and introduced himself.

"Mr. and Mrs. Downs? Here on time for your sitting. A wedding picture, isn't it?" He looked me up and down.

"Got married in your uniform, eh? You lose that in Vietnam?" He pointed to my hook.

"Yes, I did, up in I Corps." I thought nothing about the question. My hook was a curious-looking device and I was used to people asking about it.

He looked at me, nodded, and told us to follow him back to his studio. As Mary and I posed for our wedding pictures, he began to quiz me.

"You were an officer in Vietnam?" he asked me as he sat me down and walked back to his camera. Mary stood beside me, her hand on my shoulder. We were both beaming for the camera.

"Yes, a second lieutenant, infantry."

"Infantry, huh? That's pretty tough. I was in the South Pacific in World War II; just an enlisted man, though."

"Yeah, but in 'Nam in the combat unit we were in, it didn't make much difference in the jungle whether a man was an officer or enlisted. The measure was how well a guy pulled his weight."

"What about the Vietnamese? What kind of soldiers are they?"

"Oh, pretty good. They are tough soldiers."

"Must have been difficult fighting with all those women and children around."

"Well, yes, it was pretty hard but luckily we did most of our fighting up in the jungle. I hated the flat ground where the civilians were."

"What about the prisoners? I bet I know what you did with them." His voice had become higher and more strident. "I'll tell you what we used to do with Jap prisoners in the Islands. The same thing you did with the Vietnamese; we threw them out of airplanes like you did the Vietnamese out of helicopters."

I didn't like the way this conversation was going but I felt I had to say something.

"Welllll, we never threw anyone out of a helicopter. I don't know anyone who did. I think those are just war stories."

"Oh, don't kid me, Lieutenant!" He stressed the word lieutenant as he came around in front of his camera. "I used to be a soldier. I know what we did and you can't tell me any different!"

This guy was serious! I looked at my wife. She was just

as puzzled. After all, we were here to have our wedding picture taken, not to talk about war and prisoners and killing.

He pressed his attack, "How does it feel to kill a woman?"

"What?"

"You heard me, Lieutenant! It's in all the news broadcasts how you are killing innocent civilians—women, children, and old men over there. We never did that. All we fought were Japs."

"Wait a minute—the enemy we fought is just as tough as any soldier. And besides, we didn't go around killing innocent civilians on purpose, for God's sake!"

"On purpose, eh! Bet you killed plenty accidentally on purpose, didn't you? You Vietnam guys are all whining and crying about the big bad war when all you've been fighting are civilians in a civil war."

"*No*, you are wrong! A lot of good Americans died over there fighting the Communists, and I'm telling you we did not wantonly kill any civilians. I lost a lot of friends in that fighting."

"Oh sure, and I suppose you're going to tell me that you were fighting to save America too? You are a joke. You and all of those soldiers don't deserve to be called Americans! I belong to the American Legion and every man there served his country proudly. You Vietnam guys wouldn't make a wart on their ass."

My stomach was churning. Cold waves of shock washed through me. My God, I thought of the men who had been killed, who had been *killed*, and those who had been wounded, their lives shattered, and the pride I felt as an American soldier. I looked in horror at this vicious man spouting hate and accusations at me.

At me! I had done what my country asked. All of us in Vietnam were as good at soldiering as anybody else. This man was reaching out to soil our lives.

I had paid my price in an American war. I now belonged, a disabled veteran, one of those special people, in my romantic view of the war, who automatically gained the respect of his fellow citizens because of the sacrifice he had made. I turned to answer, "I don't think you're right. There are. . . ."

"What? More fools like you who can't fight and don't belong there anyway? It's so-called men like you who are ruining America's reputation in the world because you can't find, much less beat, the Vietcong, so you just shoot at anything that walks."

I turned to Mary. "Let's go." Rage, frustration, and a terrible feeling of betrayal had pushed me to the edge emotionally.

Why had I survived the war only to return to a country which treated me like shit? That anti-war stuff on television was one thing, but this was a personal attack on me.

I was in a daze as Mary guided me out of the door. On the drive up Colfax Avenue returning home, I began to shake. When I got into the house I went back to my room where I stood again before the mirror. Tears came and would not stop, spasms of hurt deeper than wounds. Fifteen years have passed. Yet I can picture myself today, in 1983, as if it were yesterday—standing in my room, gazing through tears at the mirror's reflection of a gaunt soldier sobbing in shuddering heaves. Somehow the crying should not fit the man standing in a bedecked uniform, a uniform which represented strength, duty, and honor. Yet the crying, the man, and the uniform were the same.

Such hate I felt toward the photographer. I should have hit him. But that would have proved his point. Still, I should have struck him, I should have killed him; I will go back and hit him, kill him, destroy his business, hunt his family down and kill them. . . . No! No! No! You are confused; that is lowering yourself to his level, you are a better man than he.

You have seen enough of death and misery. This photographer is sick, stay away from him; you were right to walk away.

Mary stood in the doorway, crying helplessly, watching me cry as I said between sobs, "I don't understand. Why did he do that? I gave it my all, my men died, those months in the hospital, the death, agony, and all of those people. They were good men . . . and . . . no one understands!! Jesus Christ, what has gone wrong?"

In my mind's eye I was in a foxhole behind an M-60 machine gun facing a tree line. The photographer appeared in front.

I pulled the cocking mechanism back, squeezed the trigger, and sprayed him with a fire burst of machine-gun rounds. Pieces of his head and body were ripped away by the force of the rounds. I crawled out of the foxhole, stood up, and walked over to where his body lay. I looked down at him and felt satisfaction at his death. I had destroyed him the way I had destroyed so many in the hospitals.

I shook my head out of the reverie and looked up at my tear-streaked face in the mirror. I did not look like a destroyer; I looked like the sad, troubled young man I was. All of my beliefs about honor, pride, duty, and country were being trampled by anti-war protesters whom I saw on television, by newspaper columnists and editorials I read, and, most confusing of all, by some senators and representatives who were part of the government that led us into Vietnam in the first place. Christ! I was the only man in my platoon old enough to vote for God's sake! How could they even consider holding us responsible?

People were demanding that we soldiers take a stand. Admit that Vietnam was wrong, that we were all a bunch of kill-crazy psychos. People were demanding that we accept this tremendous guilt about Vietnam, wear ashes, and go out among the masses confessing our sins so the public could be justified in their belief that they were right about us all along.

The pressure was intense. It never let up, no matter where we were. Whether I was talking to one person or at a gathering of people, the subject of Vietnam would come up. I would be asked my opinion and attacked immediately when I did not answer the way they thought I should.

Finally, there was no relief in any answer. One faction condemned me because I was a soldier and tainted—unless I did as some soldiers did, admit guilt. Some soldiers responded so eagerly to the anti-war protests that they were accepted into that group, even idolized. They had seen the light but to do so and maintain their credibility they had to shun any soldier who had not confessed error.

On the other hand, the other factions seemed to believe the media claims that we were not good as soldiers because we could not win the war and were, in addition, corrupted with drugs, alcohol, criminal activities, and cheap sex in Saigon. We were portrayed as losers. We had let America down.

As a result, we were shoved into limbo, claimed by neither side and blamed by both.

So there I was—the bastards! I hated them all! I slammed my fist into the door jamb next to the mirror; shafts of pain up the arm cleared my mind!

The soldier in the mirror checked out my uniform. "Fuck them!" I resolved I would never apologize for my action in Vietnam. I was proud to be a soldier, proud of my platoon, proud to be an American. They will never take that away from me!

Tears caused by the hurt inside my spirit and by the futility of it all continued to cascade down my cheeks. Mary hugged me tightly to give me solace. She was as puzzled as I was as to what was happening.

"All those men killed and wounded," I sobbed. "They meant something to me. They weren't what these people back here are implying. And besides, the war is over for us now."

"No," Mary replied. "I don't think so. I don't think the war will ever be over for you. They won't let it be over."

I stared over her shoulder at my tear-stained face reflected in the mirror. I didn't have an answer.

April 1975: South Vietnam Unconditionally Surrenders

The major spring offensive by the North Vietnamese Army had surprised the world with its success. I had avidly watched television every day and night as the South Vietnamese military folded in on itself as the North Vietnamese rushed south toward Saigon.

I watched the end approach with a dark foreboding. I identified strongly with the success or failure of South Vietnam. I had a vested interest in the country because it had affected and changed my whole life. I could not ignore its fate. My blood and the blood of my friends had darkened its soil. No matter how melodramatic this sounds, it was literally impossible for me to discount the price we had paid for the welfare of South Vietnam.

And now it all seemed for naught. What a heavy burden of loss weighed me down as the faces of my friends and platoon members kept intruding in my thoughts.

The pictures on television of the "Huey" helicopters piloted by South Vietnamese, hovering above the sea next to American ships while the people on board the chopper jumped into the sea, were terrible.

But the most disheartening sight was when the pilot deliberately lowered his craft into the water. Invariably it would tilt to the left and a rotor blade tip would touch the water causing the blade to torque and bend like a living thing.

The chopper would lurch and shudder from the whipping, physical twisting of the moving parts disintegrating from the powerful horsepower engine, forcing the unbalanced machinery into a death spasm as it sank in the blink of an eye beneath the waves. The machine's violent, ignoble end always shocked me.

I would be on the edge of my seat, pulled close to the screen so I would miss no details. I would not relax until the pilot's head popped up to the surface. A man that brave deserved to live.

But strange to me was the helicopter's destruction representing the end of the fighting in Vietnam. The big, ugly, ungainly looking machine was made in America, performed mightily in its tasks both in combat and as a Medivac, and, in its final duty, the South Vietnamese had dumped it into the sea after perfecting their escape.

Yeah, I felt we had both been used.

On the afternoon of 29 April 1975, I was driving north on I-25, the valley highway, in Denver. The setting sun was reflecting from hundreds of window squares in the office buildings in downtown Denver. The snow-capped Continental Divide stretched in a high rugged line along the brilliantly blue sky. A white stream of clouds hugged the two mountain peaks to the north, Long and Meeker.

Country and western music was playing on the car radio and I was paying particular attention to the music and the road as I thought of the Cessna 172 I would be flying in in an hour from Broomfield Airport.

The music ended and the announcer stated that he had an important message for the listeners. I turned my attention to the radio and heightened the volume.

The announcer read the teletype statement that South Vietnam had just surrendered unconditionally to the North Vietnamese. The war was over!

All thoughts became mish-mashes of flashbacks of Vietnam. I stared in shock at the road in front of me as I slowed the car. Although I had been expecting South Vietnam to fall, I was astonished at the depth of sadness and loss I felt.

I looked over at the mountains and thought of Bob Hutchinson. He would probably be surfing now if he had not been killed in Vietnam seven years ago.

What a strange thought to strike me out of all the others.

I had unconsciously slowed almost to a stop. The announcer in a solemn voice said, "In honor of the American men who lost their lives in Vietnam and to those men and women who served in Vietnam, this station will now play *The Star-Spangled Banner.*"

Goosebumps rose all over my body as I cried unashamedly during the anthem. Tears were all I could give to my friends in memory of their suffering and deaths.

When the anthem ended I shut off the radio and noticed that I was parked alongside the road. Traffic rushed by, oblivious. I dimly realized that I had to drive on.

I pulled back onto the road and drove into the foothills, where I stopped and looked back over the plains that rose from the Mississippi Valley nine hundred miles away to touch the edge of the mountains at my feet. I looked over my shoulder at the mountain peaks. I sat down, leaned back against a rock, and breathed deeply. My tears were done.

I wondered if my country would ever welcome us back. Welcome all of us in body and in spirit.

Or would we always remain a flaw in America's vision of itself.

MEN AT WAR!

Gritty, gutsy, fascinating, real, here are stories of World War II and Vietnam— -and the men who fought in them.

_____	**THE KILLING ZONE:**	06534-0/$3.50
	MY LIFE IN THE VIETNAM WAR	
	Frederick Downs	
_____	**AFTERMATH**	07564-8/$3.50
	Frederick Downs	
_____	**NAM**	07168-5/$3.50
	Marc Baker	
_____	**SEMPER FI, MAC**	06253-8/$3.95
	Henry Berry	

Prices may be slightly higher in Canada.

Available at your local bookstore or return this form to:

BERKLEY
Book Mailing Service
P.O. Box 690, Rockville Centre, NY. 11571

Please send me the titles checked above. I enclose _____ Include 75¢ for postage and handling if one book is ordered; 25¢ per book for two or more not to exceed $1.75. California, Illinois, New York and Tennessee residents please add sales tax.

NAME _____

ADDRESS _____

CITY _____ STATE/ZIP _____

(allow six weeks for delivery.)